Life
AFTER
LIGHTNING

A JOURNEY OF SPIRITUAL AND SELF DISCOVERY

BETH PETERSON

Life
AFTER
LIGHTNING

A JOURNEY OF SPIRITUAL AND SELF DISCOVERY

BETH PETERSON

diamondstudded treetoes
Mount Vernon, Iowa
www.diamondstuddedtreetoes.com

diamondstudded treetoes
P.O. Box 37 Mount Vernon, Iowa 52314
Copyright © 2013 Beth Peterson

Published in the United States
Second Edition 11 10 9 8 7 6 5 4 3 2

Library of Congress Cataloging-in-Publication Data
Peterson, Beth
Life After Lightning
by Beth Peterson, 2nd Edition
ISBN-978-0-9860551-0-2 (2nd Edition HC)
Printed In Canada
p. cm.

Book Design and Editing by Cole Norton
2nd Edition Editing by Jillian Rutledge

DEDICATION

This book is dedicated to my husband Dave. You are my true person and I appreciate you standing beside me while I gathered the broken pieces of me. You have given me the freedom to accomplish the things that I came back here to do. I love you for that. My children, Angela and Casey, follow your dreams and live your passion! I love you both with all my heart and even when you think I'm not looking, I see you. Remember, moms have eyes in the back of their heads! To all my friends and family who never stopped believing in me, I have never given up on my dreams; I just took the long road around the universe to accomplish them. It really doesn't matter how many treacherous roads I have had to walk to get here, I will be forever grateful to all of you that have crossed my path on my journey. My aunt Spirit Wolf, you guided me through my most darkest days and I love you for teaching me to trust in the plans of the universe. You gave me my wings back and taught me to follow the path that was lit up with my light. Without you, I don't think I would be where I am. Mom and Dad, the, paths that you each chose gave me a lesson to learn and an experience to

I

experience. Without them, I would not have been able to become who I was meant to be. My life was never easy, but our family circumstances were what gave me my strength to survive. Mom, I feel your whispers of "I love you," from heaven. Dad, "The Nnelgster", you will always be my best friend and I love you too! Karen Hackman-Peterson, thanks for being the best mom-in-law I could have ever dreamed of having. You have made me see a different side of kindness and love. You support me in all my odd ways. Aunt Karla "Baby" Williams, I could write a whole book on how much you showed me as a child. You were my connection to the stars in the sky. I never forgot to look up and keep dreaming. Lisa Barta, you taught me patience and to always wear sequins in the morning. You helped me understand that some people need more time to see their light and to not give up on them too soon. "What the heck are you doing?" and "Wake up!" became life lessons in themselves, but we finally connected the dots of our picture and now we are coloring it in. Angelena Madsen, the truest angel on Earth, I have been blessed to know you. You have the most genuine kindness and compassion of anyone I have ever crossed paths with. Others could take a lesson from you, my friend. Ryan McCombs, Adam Zadel and Tim King, my biggest dream ever was teaching you to believe in your meant to be, as it gave me the confidence to believe in my own. I am so proud of your perseverance. Dr. Ann Sadler, thanks for letting me start with baby steps. In my heart, I am running a marathon now! My long lost friends, "Chipper," A.K.A. Steve Elwood, Alex Ross, and Mary Pea, thanks for not forgetting me. My grandpas, Jack Sharp and Floyd McNelly, both Veterans to our Great Nation, you two were the best inspiration. I miss you both, but I know that you can see me from heaven. My Grandmother, Bonnie McNelly, yes, I know, that you are proud, heaven is only a veil between us. My Grandma Marie Sharp, thank you for being my Grandma, even when you didn't have to. I love you for accepting me into your life. Tammi Delaney and Shari Jones, we are Sisters Three. My time with you both is worth my return to

Earth. I love you and am proud of the women you have become. Always remember to spread your wings and fly, like the butterfly. Shane Delaney and Rick Jones, my sisters are blessed to have such wonderful spouses to walk their journey with. My sisters-in-law, Christine Melichar, Kelly Peterson, and Michelle Stafford, I love you all. Robyn Netz (neighbor), no matter how far you go, you will always be one of my strangest friends! Chris Rutledge, Kate Williams, Kim Steele, Mary Martin, and Loretta Conner, thanks for being my friends. God works in such fabulous ways to bring all of you into my life the many times that I have needed some extra love. You all rock! Michelle Bakke, my hair color queen, well you have worked your own miracles on me! Elias Soriano, I'm glad my wings were dry by the time I met you. Gary and Patty McCool, your kindness is inspiring and your prayers with us to Jesus Christ gave us peace, lifted us up, and helped us heal. To all of you, as well as any I may have forgotten to mention, I love you all. My journey would not be as enlightening as it has been without each person who has connected a dot in the picture of my life. I am honored and grateful to have crossed paths with each of you. Let the journey continue.

~~~

LIFE AFTER LIGHTNING

INTRODUCTION

Have you ever wondered about the purpose of your life? It is something I have pondered often. I have experienced so many different things in this lifetime, seen so many places, met so many people. I am only left to wonder, what could be the connection of it all? The choices we make and the paths we choose all seem to have a meaning, leading us toward one ultimate purpose.

In my mind's eye, I imagine that my life path looks something like an overgrown, old growth oak tree. I have so many branches reaching outward, some paths taken and some yet to be traveled. I have been battered and bruised, twisted and cracked, hit by a couple bolts of lightning, and yet I still stand strong. My bark is weathered and my roots are never too deep. I have to keep them shallow and only deep enough to stay standing. If I were to let them grow too deep I would grow too much attachment to my surroundings, possibly not allowing myself to move on towards the next experience of my journey; the experience that my soul recognizes, that next meant to be moment on my path. So I keep myself going through the seasons and cycles of my life trying to make the connection, and ultimately, find the answer to it all.

I have loved, and I have been loved as well. I have also been abused, beyond any want of those memories. Through every victimizing experience put upon me, although I have survived, the memories still remain. I have been blessed to feel the love and light of God completely engulf me. A love that does not compare to anything in this physical life form. It was a different kind of love that encompassed me in the brightest, most spectacular light that I have ever seen. It covered me with the deepest knowing, that I was not a forgotten soul, but one child of God with a connection to the other side and to that one great spiritual being who had felt my pain. All of it. Every moment that I felt I would not be able to live through, He was feeling my pain.

I was born to be a survivor! I have had just as many victimizing experiences as I have had extraordinary ones in my lifetime; each one of them for a reason. Every one of them to give me an understanding. All of them, memories not forgotten. Why? So that I would survive to help you...

When I set out to write this book, I had one goal in mind. I had to make it a book to pay it all forward. This book is meant to inspire you to be a survivor. It's to teach you to believe in the person that you may only dream of being. I want to show you a better way of living, not just existing in your life in a victim role. After everything I have survived I have learned one very important thing: I am meant to do great things. For if I weren't, I would not still be alive. I would have died when I was hit by that first bolt of lightning. Now, I don't want anyone to think that their life journey has to be as astounding as mine, for each of us has a different path to walk. Each of us has a journey that is our own. We each have lessons; it is our destiny to find the answers to them and unlock the secrets of what we need to learn. I walk in my own light of knowing that I will find the answers that I seek. I have an unearthly connection to a highly spiritual belief. I am frustrated that time is wasted on self-help teachings that are full of information and seem to contain no answers and no map of direction. I wanted tools to assist me on a path to wellness; tools that I was unable to find in any book and so I gathered them from my life journey of lessons and started sharing them with everyone around me. I quickly realized that I could talk all day, but if the words I say don't leave you with some tools to make progress, then why waste your time and my breath. My goal is to share with you the tools that I have gathered and give to you some easy ways to make yourself aware of your time, your purpose in life, and the beauty and wonder of you. I want to help you unload the baggage of unnecessary things we tend to carry around with us in life.

My path to wellness was not an easy one to travel. In truth, it took me years to build a network of people whom I could trust to have my best interests in the forefront of their mind. In my opinion, every person seeking help should be looked at as a unique and individual human being. It is very unfortunate that we are all looked at as groups in a text book. I am my own person, different from most, and yet I have found ways to make my life, and many other peoples lives, better. I find it much more healing to work on a person's past hurts, instead of medicating a persons mind where one becomes numb to the emotions they have experienced. Life is a journey of happiness and hurts. Without those hurts we would not learn the skills that we need to become better, stronger souls. We each have a purpose, a path of life events to experience.

As you set forth into this book of truth, do not feel sorry for me, for I have only endured the experiences that were meant for me to survive. Without them, I would not be able to understand, or even relate to, the painful things that you have had to face on your journey. I hope that together we can gather some of the tools needed for you to learn your lessons and really live your life.

~~~

LIFE AFTER LIGHTNING

NOTE TO READERS

Do not be afraid to live your life to the fullest potential that you can imagine. The growth you achieve and feel after completing your first step in your right direction will feel amazing. Each positive change you make will feed your soul and give you a new definition to the meaning of you. As you define and redefine the person whom you want to be, you will persevere into that realm with a new sense of self-worth. An incredible sense of enlightenment shall wash over you. You are somebody! Live your passion. Believe in your dreams. Never, ever, give up. It is time for you to make yourself proud.

After my visit to the other side, I have a more enlightened view on life, death, and living. I have been blessed to learn about many different religions, spiritual beliefs, and Native American cultures. I have gained knowledge and understanding from each of these and have found that we are all connected in so many ways. After experiencing my own death, I was given a choice to stay on the other side or return to this Earth plane and help others on their journey and path to fulfillment. I am in no way saying that my belief is the only belief. It is what I experienced, learned from, and ultimately survived. My hope is that I can share a few of my survival lessons with you and help you find a connection to your inner power which resides within you. To give you something to connect with your God, your Great Spirit, your Creator. To find your best path of learning and achieving all that you were meant to be from walking on this Earth. We come from a vast universe and we have a purpose with a plan for our own individual soul's growth. Life was never meant to be a cake walk. You are here for a reason. You are going through your lessons for a purpose. God feels everything that you are feeling. Allow yourself to find your true identity. Seek your meant to be destiny and walk that path. The true you is waiting for you to decide.

My only desire is for each individual to take from this book what they feel a connection to. I am only sharing the lessons I have experienced and gathered knowledge from. I want you to be able to insert the God balance that best suits your faith, for it is not up to me to judge any living soul on this planet. We each have a purpose with a lesson to learn and I would never be the judge of who is right or wrong in their beliefs. I am only responsible for my own choices and consequences in my lifetime. It is up to each of us to be and become the best individual soul we can with the pieces that we gather from our own experiences. I have dear friends of many different religion-based faiths, spiritual-based beliefs, and native cultures. We all have great things to bring to the conversation and we allow each other to be open and honest, without judgement of each other. One of the most enlightening pieces of knowledge I came back with from my experience of death was that I should never judge another human being. That is not a right given to any of us. Yet, I encounter people of many faiths who are quick to judge the ones who do not believe in or follow their faith. If this is you step back, you are not God. You are made from him. Therefore, you have an obligation to be a wiser person and be forgiving, just as God is with you. It is not for you to be the judge. If you want others to be inspired by you and your beliefs, try leading by example. The best way to be a leader is to be inspiring to those who cross your path. Remember, the only person you have the ability to change is you. Be the best, most inspiring, non-judgmental, person you can be. That is what will attract others to be more like you and give them the inspiration to want to change themselves.

~~~

Everything in life happens for a reason. Every person who crosses your path is connected to you in some way, for some purpose. Sometimes we connect the dots, other times, we refuse to see. My only hope is that you can be inspired by something inside these pages since everything I have survived has a connection to a reason.

Always, Beth

LIFE AFTER LIGHTNING

INDEX

~1~

SHINE

Shine your light
Down on me
I need confirmation
I'm where I'm meant to be
To choose my path wisely
But see
With a crystal clear vision
That where I am going
Is where my soul
Can be free
I walk in the light of knowing
That I am meant to do great things
To always help guide others
When my own answers don't come cheap
Life is a circle
Sometimes a crooked path
The end result is experience
Every one meant to last
So when I need your light
It's just to help me see
Through those heart heavy moments
I feel a little broken
And empty
Pick me up
Stand me back on my feet
I'll be all right
After your light
Shines down on me

We all have moments of need. Times when we are searching for the meaning of our own existence. A lack of strength inside to help us see the next step our feet need to take. Clarity can seem so far out of focus that we feel alone. Life is so much easier to see after stepping outside of the emotion of any situation. Even I have had trouble seeing the answers to my dilemmas while I am standing in the midst of them. I try to remind myself to look at the situation from an outside point of view; like looking at it through a window, it helps to take a look in a different light. It helps you to gain a different perspective on your current situation. When I am feeling down or frustrated I remind myself of the journey I am on, which is the path that God has set in front of me. I try to look at the lesson to find my connection and gain the knowledge necessary to add meaning to my existence. I have faith; faith in knowing that in this vast universe there is a plan for me. I know I am walking in the light of God and that it is His light that ultimately shines down on me.

Even through all of my broken experiences, the pain I have endured, and the times that I have survived it all to live another day, I have not lost my faith. I am able to remind myself that a plan is in place. As soon as I allow myself to learn the lesson which has been put in place for me, I can move forward out of that experience. I do not have to let the pain of the situation define me, but let it be a part of what shapes me into who I am. If I were to allow a painful situation to consume my thoughts I would spend more time wasting energy and turning myself in circles without gaining the knowledge needed to gather what I have to learn to help me move forward. If it helps, look at life as a video game. You are trying to reach the next level but without gathering the pieces needed, you aren't allowed to move on. So gather them, tuck them into your invisible satchel, throw them over your shoulder and move on to the next level God and the universe has placed in front of you. You have the power inside of you to accomplish anything you set your positive mind to do.

Stop complicating things in your own life. As you gain the positive power in your mind it will feed the spirit inside you. As your spiritual growth is fed you become balanced, stronger, and more capable of being in harmony with the journey you are meant to be walking. When the day comes that you realize the progress you are making simply because you stopped complicating and manipulating your own growth, acknowledge and validate it. Allow yourself to reflect on the changes you have made. Revisit your past, but only long enough to remember where you came from. If it helps keep a notebook, journal, a sticky note pad, whatever you need, something to jot down the changes you are making. Thumbing back through them will help you see your actual footsteps on the path that you have chosen. Seeing your changes, on paper and within, will encourage you to share what you have learned with others. How attractive you may become to others is an interesting thing to realize. Not in physical beauty, but in your attitude, demeanor and the way you carry yourself with more confidence. Your personal and positive changes will create a brighter light that burns around you. It is that light I speak of in this poem. I felt this light pour over me when I passed to the other side. It is that light of God which filled me to overflowing just before I came back to Earth, back into my body.

Remember, while you are making this transitional change to find that better part of you, give thanks and know that you are never alone. You are walking in God's light as it shines down on you. Take the time to acquaint yourself with it. It is a priceless gift from above. As changes take place in your life a shift in consciousness occurs. You will become more aware of the positive energy that connects you to others who are like you. Together, we will be able to make this world a better place.

We have become a society that wants everyone around us to tell us what to do next. We want someone else to fix our pain, relationships, careers, and so forth. Trust yourself, you know you better than anyone else. Stop seeking out opinions; they only serve as your next excuse to not move forward. Life and living are up to you. You hold your own play book. What you choose to create while walking your life journey ultimately connects your life book in the afterlife. Everything you do will connect to something that someone else has done or is doing. That is how I know that we have the power to create change. When I stood on the other side and saw my book of life I was able to see the connection of every person who had ever walked through my life. I had the choice, at every moment, to change the course of my life path.

If you are reading this and feel it is time for you to wake up and change the direction you have been traveling, then welcome! Now, lets get moving! Change is waiting for you!

~~~

Celebrate, love, and embrace yourself.

~2~

GRIEF

Drowning
Current carries me
To another place
Only to roll me under with the tide
Spit me up
Through the next crashing wave
As I hit the shore
I try to stand
On the coarse, wet sand
Try to get my balance
Only to be pulled back down
Into the darkness, again
Wish that I could fly
High above it all
Watch from a safe distance
Though I can't seem to keep my wings dry
From all my tears being shed
An ocean full

This is how I felt the day my mother was diagnosed with stage four, untreatable, metastatic cancer. I could hardly breath. My mind seemed to have disconnected from my body's ability to move. I felt as though I were drowning or as if I was being rolled under into the oceans surf. All I could picture were the wet wings of an angel, unable to fly out of this tragic moment in time. I felt as though I should have seen this coming so I could help prepare her for this terrible turn in her life. She always looked to me for answers, but this time, I had none. Just when we were getting her life to a place of beautiful dreams with endless possibilities, this hit us like that giant crashing wave. I wanted to wake up and have it be a really bad dream. I wanted to scream. I wanted to run. Anything to get us away from the reality of what we were being told. Mom was looking at me, expecting me to right this situation and believing I would come up with a reasonable way of fixing this. At that moment, she took my hand and asked me what we were going to do. The only thing that slipped through my numb mind, and crossed my dry lips was, "don't you worry, Mom. We will figure this out." My heart was breaking and life as we knew it was forever going to be changed.

I had no idea what on Earth I was going to do! I replayed it so many times in my mind. I saw how scared she was. I held her soft, aging hand. I felt the cold chill of her imminent death flow between us. Right then, I decided that I wanted answers. I went searching for solutions to questions nobody seemed to have any answers to. How did this happen? What can we do to fix it? How long? What do we expect? When will things change? What should we look for? I quickly realized that we were somewhat on our own. Cancer is cancer, but each case is unique, just as each individual is different. So our lives became an interesting cycle of events. I went into a mode of "Cancer numbness." I tried to fix it the only way I could figure out how. I started getting everything in order for my mother. Notifying family and friends was first on the list. A support team is, by far, your number one priority. Set it up and make a schedule for your team to help you. There are times when five things may need to be done at once. Your team will be ready to gear up for this battle with you. It takes delegation in order for everything to not fall onto one strong persons shoulders. When help is offered, take it. When friends and neighbors tell you to call if you need anything, do it. Set up meals to be delivered and welcome friends to sit and share some quality time. It all comes down to knowing that without this network, the entire unit can be broken.

From the very first moment at the doctor's office when Mom and I found out what was wrong, we started making memories that counted. I didn't know it then, but our healing began in those early hours. It was as though God planned every second of our lives just so we could survive that moment.

I began to ask, what had my mother never got to do? What were her dreams? Her desires? When her doctor said, "Let her have whatever makes her happy," she meant, if she wanted a cheeseburger at midnight, give her a cheeseburger at midnight. If she wants a margarita, heck, let her have two! Well, I had other ideas. I was determined to make any dreams she had come true.

So it began. We gathered a small group of family and friends. We toasted her life with love and margaritas! That day my mother had her first ride on a Harley, with my husband Dave. Her arms were wrapped around him so tight, and the smile on her face will never be forgotten! That is where the memory making began and continued on each day thereafter. We took her to the Field of Dreams. We played baseball and took photos of all of us coming out of the cornfields, acting like we were really a part of the movie. We took her out and had a picnic in the rain at Palisades Park. We had dinner at sunset on The Historical Sutliff Bridge. We took her to tour a mansion. She had never imagined getting to see the inside of a home that grand and amazing. We went to the Lady Luck Casino on the Mississippi River. Mom was the only lucky lady in our group that day. We had bonfires and food with friends and family. We had a local musician come to play and sing, just for her. Imagine, her own private concert! She sat there, front and center, smiling through every song. We wanted her to know how special she was to so many people.

She had family come from California, Washington, Oregon, Arizona, and Georgia. At one time we had 30 people at her tiny apartment. Now, it is important that I give thanks to her landlord. We could not have pulled this off without him. I'm sure some over occupancy rules were bent or broken, for us. He even allowed visitors to set up their tents in the big back yard. What a wonderful person. We could not imagine having a kinder landlord on this Earth. He even came to pray with Mom. He talked to her and prepared her for Heaven. He had to have recognized the wonderfully beautiful soul we all knew her to be.

As her days turned into weeks we all settled into our routines and responsibilities. We designated duties that suited each of our strengths. We functioned like a group of young women on a mission from God. We knew the more we did to make her cancer life more comfortable, the smoother her transition out of this world would be.

When she was no longer able to leave the apartment for our planned field trip outings, we brought the memories to her. We had a photographer come and take pictures outside. The photos looked like we were in a studio. They turned out beautiful! There were so many amazing people who dropped off meals, donated supplies, and offered hugs for support. People would come by just to sit and spend time with her. It was as if they knew the world would feel her absence. She had an inspirational effect on people. She was a friend whom people could count on. She always showed kindness and compassion to all she met.

As the seasons went by hospice came to prepare us, if there was such a thing. All I can tell you is that we ended up teaching our hospice team how three daughters could change a tragedy into a daily celebration of one person's life.

Oh yes! We dressed up for Halloween and trick-or-treated our mom. We decorated a tree in September for Christmas, just in case she wasn't with us. I'm so glad we did since we lost her four days before the holiday. Mom had so many gifts to unwrap; I bet it took her an hour! The hospice people thought we were crazy at first. They never knew what holiday they were going to walk into at Mom's apartment. It was so magical. Only God knew what was taking place underneath all the emotions that were rolling over us, like waves in the ocean.

It still amazes me how three daughters, three sisters, three friends, were able to rebuild a bond with our mother. We were also able to build her an amazing sand castle of dreams, like a fairytale, in one tiny apartment overflowing with love and cancer.

~~~

First, meditate. Center your energy.

Prepare your mind and visualize.

Walk yourself through your situation.

Take extra time to empower yourself, whether it be

hair, makeup, clothing, jewelry, or your attitude.

Feel confident in yourself.

That way, you aren't stressing over something that you can't

control. The empowerment starts within. Being prepared leaves

less up to chance.

~3~

WONDER

How would it be
If I couldn't be me
To have nothing
To laugh at
From the depths
With no glee
Throw my arms in the air
Shout out to all
I am free
Only to realize
That only sisters
Strong and faithful
Can see
The forever
Never ending
Connection of life
The power of three
Not distance
Nor time
Was able
To break
The bond
Of she in me
I only wonder
What one thinks
When she looks down
On three

As you know, we lost our Mother on December 21, 2007, to metastatic cancer at age 57. However, we were given those four glorious months to make every day a magical memory. To say it was a tremendous gift of time would be a complete understatement. It was one of the most rewarding experiences of my life, as my two sisters and I had moved in with her. Not just one at a time, but all three of us together, in her two bedroom apartment. How blessed we were to have the support systems that we did in our own homes from our own families. It meant so much to each of us that we were supported in our decision to give our mother an unselfish gift, our time. We devoted ourselves to showing her how deeply she was loved. We allowed ourselves to take that time away from our own families and devote it to her care. I know it wasn't just for my mother, but also for three sisters to seal a bond. For us to know that we would still have each other when our mother was gone. Going through an experience like that can test so many parts of you from your emotions, to your sanity, to your spiritual beliefs, and to the very core of who you are as a person. It can take every confidence you've ever had and spit it right back into your own face. It makes you question God, it makes you question humanity and, most of all, it makes you question your own ability to survive it. We each had lessons to learn on the path of our mother's disease.

So, we did the only thing we knew how to do. We made a plan to survive and to come out on the other side of this experience with no regrets and nothing left undone. After all, we were three sisters, wise enough to realize that the ones left behind to grieve are the ones who can ultimately suffer the most. That was not going to be us! We were going to help our mother live through the time that she had left, laugh through the deep eating pain, and love her through all the horrid side affects that came along with this ugly disease. We were going to show her that we loved her like she had never been loved before! We wanted her to feel the blessings of her life, the same blessings in which she sacrificed so much of her own self, always giving to others. We chose not see the disease as a monster, even though we all knew it was. We decided to survive and conquer that big ugly thing called Cancer! Make no mistake though, our mother was not going to beat this disease. It was growing and thriving in masses throughout her entire body, including seven tumors in her brain. However, she raised us to know that we could survive anything, even her Cancer! So, the wonder in this poem is the fact that three sisters managed to create so many blessings out of something that had the potential to leave us wounded in devastating heartache. I can only smile as I wonder what our mother thinks of us as she looks down from Heaven at three grown women who learned to celebrate her life while we were given an opportunity of a lifetime. We did not let this experience turn into tragedy and did not let it destroy our lives. On the contrary, we looked at it as a four month moment of divine intervention. We look at it as a gift from above and an experience on this journey we call life.

There is not one moment of our time together that I would ever want to change. In four short months, as we were making her unafraid of death, she was creating a network for us to carry on in life and inspiring us to choose a path to help others. She lifted us up with undeniable strength by showing us that she was not afraid to go home to God and all those who had passed before her.

If I could give you some advice it would be to make those memories, create them while you still have the opportunity, take the time to make every minute count, and leave no room for regrets. Time with a loved one is a unique gift. Work it into your schedule. This is something you should not procrastinate. The grief you feel in the end is more often felt from the guilt. I guarantee that you will heal faster after your loved one's passing if you gift yourself, and them, with a little bit of your personal time. Make your memories. Make every day count and bask in the knowing that we are never really out of their sight, not even from heaven.

~~~

Today, I choose to see the wonder in me.

~4~

TOUCH

I felt her skin
With my hands
Impress into my memory
Make my mind
Along with my fingers
Feel
I want to recall it
When I need to
I felt her hair
I smelled her scent
Pray I will never forget
These small details
Remembering these things
So that I recognize
Her touch
Her energy
From a place far away
When it reaches through
A veil
That separates
Our time and existence
To brush across my soul
With the softest whispers
Of I love you

We settled into a strange routine of preparation for our mothers passing with the duties divided between us. Each of our individual duties were designated to best take care of our mother. It also gave each of us our own time with her. It became a reality that any day could be her last. I think it helped to not have one person feel overwhelmed by how much needed to be done.

As each day passed and we began to get into the swing of our new routines, new responsibilities, and our new understanding of cancer, I became increasingly more thoughtful of the things I needed to remember about my mother. Her touch, her smell, the sound of her voice, the sensation of her energy, her soul, and the true spiritual essence of who she really was. Most importantly, I paid attention to my own intuition. I was becoming increasingly aware that time was running out. I found myself staring at her, just to memorize her. I wanted to remember everything there was to know about her. I touched her face, rubbed the soft skin on her hands, felt her hair. We hugged, we talked, we asked questions. We got answers. Nothing was off limits. We gave her every bit of who we had each grown up to become. I do believe we can communicate with those on the other side. Either through dreams or just that angel touch across your cheek. I tuned myself into her energy. We balanced with each other in mind, body, and spirit.

Now when I get that feeling or feel that touch of energy surrounding me from out of the blue or in a dream, driving down the road, or listening to a song, I know that I recognize it. I had memorized it. I embrace it back. I share those moments with her as I feel those softly whispered feelings saying, "I love you." Then, I thank God. We were all blessed with the time we needed to accomplish so much. We don't know why, we don't know how, and we certainly can't say who felt more blessed, us or her. Like an intersection of life, that street ran both ways.

The stark reality of life is the factual truth that one day death will befall each and every one of us. The mission, so to speak, is to figure out a way to exist blessedly after the loss of someone close to you. The truth is, the ones left here to grieve sometimes suffer more than the ones who've passed from tragedy, illness, or by other means. It is up to us to find that bag of tools, gather what each of us needs to get through this life, and do it with as little suffering as we can. God above feels our pain, and it is not something that is a meant to be burden for any of us to carry the grief throughout our entire lifetime of existence. Feel it. Embrace it. Let it flow over you because the one thing death may be trying to teach you is to live! Live through the memories and lessons that you have experienced. Help another person who is going through it. Share your bag of tools. We are not destined to fail over grief. We are meant to rise to the occasion of it and rejoice in memories of the person you have lost. You were blessed to be so touched by the one you are grieving for. From where they stand, it is not sadness that they want you to be feeling, but happiness for them. Celebrate their transition to the other side. Enlighten your spirit with the knowledge that we are all here to help each other. Do not let grief derail your path in life.

~~~

Dear Mom,

How are things in heaven? Down here we're doing fine. The kids are fully grown now and we see them from time to time. They are doing what you told them to and their passion in life truly shines. I don't worry much about them, because I know they have a crew of Angels watching over them, and that includes You. I just wanted you to know that today you crossed my mind. I feel your absence in my daily life as I race against the time. To complete the things of my meant to be, so others can be inspired. As your essence washed right over me and I swear I felt your hand, touch my cheek and inspire me to believe in who you know, I already am. Thank you Mom for reminding me that you are only a thought away. Obviously I needed to feel your loving touch today. I love you Mom.

Love,

Me

~5~

SMILE

When the day seems long
When everything goes wrong
Take a moment, a pause
Pinpoint the cause
When you are feeling the stress
In your neck, in your chest
Take a breath, a stretch
Let the anxiety pass
The beauty of life
Is such an oversight
We forget too often
To turn to the light
Look up to the sky
Release a deep sigh
Feel that warmth on your skin
Let the feeling sink in
Allow yourself to live your life
Then smile

This just may be one of the hardest and easiest things a person can do. Stress, as we allow it, overwhelms our ability to think clearly. So, I thought, if I made a magic word for myself maybe I could snap myself out of the negative moment, that icky spot I may be standing in. When I am feeling that trigger, I simply smile. Just that split second action makes my chest, neck, shoulders, face, and head relax. Try it, then see how it makes you change your thoughts. I think it confuses the brain just quick enough to sometimes make you giggle. No worries that your friends, family, or coworkers may be a bit confused. When the time is right, share the magic word with them.

As a society that runs on overtime in every different direction, on any given day, you tend to miss out on everything magical around you. Stop whatever it is you are doing to run yourself into the ground. This is so out of control in our society and our generation, especially when we are having a difficult time with our true, meant to be productivity. We as a society are missing the most important connections in life. We are not living life to its fullest. We are trying to beat the clock at every given moment. Again, I say stop! Take an assessment of your quality time of living. When the day comes, and it will come, when you are no longer here to live your life, you cannot buy the time back at your local discount store. Time and living are great gifts that we are born and gifted with from above. It is not our choice as to when our minutes will expire, so use your time more wisely. Remind yourself and your family to relax. Spend some real quality time together. Create some heartfelt memories. It seems as though we are only making family time when we have an opening on the calendar. You must know that time moves on and we will be left standing one day, just wondering, where did it go?

I learned a very important lesson the week that my mother was diagnosed with cancer. I asked the doctor, how long? Her reply, quantity versus quality. It could be a month or it could be six. However long she had, her quality of life will run out before her quantity of time. I have never forgotten that moment. I remind myself of it often. It is a memory that serves only to remind me to live life well, to make the best of the time I am gifted with. Then, I smile because I know that she is smiling down on me. She fully understands the wisdom behind my suggestion to you.

So think about it. Change your thought filled, stressed out mind. Share the magic word and smile! You could soon find yourself surrounded by smiling people who are a little less stressed.

~~~

When in a relationship you carry a certain responsibility to yourself, and to your partner. Lack of communication is the number one complaint I hear from people. It makes me realize that we do not hear the other person. We can say that we talk, we can say that we are listening to everything our person says, but if we are not hearing the words that they are speaking, then we are truly not communicating. Try to pay better attention to what your person is really saying to you. True communication, with anyone, deserves your full attention.

~6~

AGE

Nerves wrapped tight
An action
A reaction
I don't want to fight
Heart squeezing shut
Words spoken
Rebellion
Communication failure
A roller coaster
Up, down
Where is solid ground
Love matters not
When they're in this tight spot
Moment happy
Hour angry
Was that a smile at me
Admission never to be
Not cool
Old fashioned
Then they turn 23

For any parent out there who has survived raising a teenager, I salute you! You have survived what should be the eighth wonder of the world. A magnificent wonder they are. I think we should make a new Olympics game designed only for teenagers. An eyeball rolling contest would be fabulous. Or a clothes on the floor obstacle course game so they can learn to walk, jump, and one foot hop over all the piles without breaking a bone or two.

Then I ask that million dollar question, is it possible that I was like that? We all know we were, in some form or another. Maybe, some not as much as others. It is the circle of life, the change, that marks their independence. They are unaware of the adult way to separate themselves and grow on their own, so it becomes a push away. Our brains just can't see our parents' logic until at least the age of twenty-three. Sometimes longer.

So I'll continue to be cool to everybody else's kids, except my own. Do me a favor though, someone be the cool parent to mine. Give advice, guidance, and a pat on the back along the way, but most of all, make sure they have the honest answers to the tough questions plaguing them. Life is somewhat like a network of living angels keeping watch over all, yours, mine, and ours.

I make light over the challenges of raising children, however, it has to be one of the most difficult tasks on my journey. I was somebody's child and stepchild. I have been a parent, both biological and as a stepmom. I am forever in a dumfounded state of mind. What you do today, that one thing that made that special little person hug you, thank you, and love you, may very well be the one thing tomorrow that embarrasses them or makes them think you are being too nosy or too helpful. That moment when self-independence arrives and you are no longer needed! I am unable to keep up with the moods changing like tomorrows tumultuous forecast.

As a mom, I love my children. I have encouraged them to seek out their individual passions in life fully, knowing that they can make their dreams come true.

I often speak with adults, who are unsatisfied in life with the choices they have made and wish they would have chosen something else. If you are miserable in your line of work, why would you force your children to make the same choices? It is frustrating and contradicting. We all want our children to be responsible, respectful, and successful members of society; that is the obvious goal! However, take a moment to really find out what they love in life. Help them research the avenues needed to accomplish it and help them gather the tools needed to make their dreams become their reality. Remind yourself that they have to do a job and support themselves for the duration of their lives. Allow them to make it something they have that passion for, not the one they get stuck in for a lifetime. Teach them and believe in them. Don't allow the search for their independence to become the one thing that divides you from them. Raising children doesn't have to become a battle of wills to demand who is right. If that happens, nobody wins.

~~~

Dear Children,

Give us the simple pleasure of showing our love to you. You are our sweetest gift in life and we cherish every moment that we have with you. It may seen like we worry too much or sometimes ask too much of you, but as your parents, we are only dreaming to have the best for you. You are our greatest loves, so the bond we share with you is nothing to be embarrassed of. It should inspire you to know that someday, you will love your child just as much as the parents who smothered you with their embarrassing love.

~7~

MOMENTS

These moments in time
I let slip through my mind
The blessings I feel
My encounters all real
As my wounds start to heal
The pain that runs deep
Even when
I can't seem to sleep
The happy, the sad
Even the bad
My laughter, my shame
When I can't place the blame
My gain, my loss
Life is a toss
A choice to survive
Thankful to be alive
My life has been spared
Though I still feel scared
To live, to trust
I can't be rushed
These moments in time
I let slip through my mind
Though I am not the same
Will you remember my name?

I have spent so much time going over my situation in my mind and mourning the loss of who I was before my encounter with lightning. I let the memories that remained float around in my mind with chunks, bits, and pieces missing. It was as though my life was a puzzle, but I could not make out the picture of who I was. There were too many missing pieces for me to get a clear image. I was so afraid to let people know just how much of my memory I had really lost. I was afraid they would think something was wrong with me, that I was weird, or worse yet, that I somehow had a mental problem. It was just missing pieces as a result of the trauma to my brain. My biggest fear was forgetting all of who I was and not recognizing my own self as I sought to find a way to get me back. These were very scary moments in time for me.

In this poem I allowed the loss of me into my own mind and acknowledged my own absence and began to accept that part of me was missing. One part of me felt so blessed to be alive since I then knew that God had a plan for me and yet, I was so lost and isolated in my own thoughts that I felt as though I were renting space or carrying a half empty suitcase in my own mind and body. It sounds silly now however, it was anything but silly. The encounters that I had experienced from my moment of death then returning to a body and mind, badly injured, was on the extreme side of frightening. I was told by everybody who examined me that they had no idea what to do to help me. There weren't enough people who lived from this with the same side affects and symptoms as I had. It was so complicated for doctors to figure out how to help me. I didn't have a disease that medicine could cure. I had trauma to my body and mind, but there just weren't very many ideas, no avenues of connection, for a recovery plan to fix me.

I finally had a doctor tell me the best thing I could have heard. He said, "You have been hit by lightning! We have tried all the medications for the symptoms that you have. They have not worked for you simply because you do not have a disease. You have been hit by lightning. You survived. Now, I think its time to find a way for you to live." He didn't have any directions, no map for me to follow or another person for me to talk to so that I could see what worked for somebody else. We had no idea as to how I was supposed to do this, just that he felt it was time. It was important to him that I stop having hope in being fixed medically and find a way to live physically and emotionally.

Again, I did the only thing that I knew how to do. I set my mind on a course to survive. It wasn't easy. Life changing experiences never are. Since I had chosen to come back and help people, surviving became my only option. It never crossed my mind to give up. It did cause me to wonder though, "Why would God ask me to come back here to help others in need?" He sent me back in this messed up, broken down, unable to function properly, "half a deck short" condition. I was too messed up to help me. How would I ever be able to help others? I was so confused! It eventually started making sense to my mind. In time, it became very clear what was happening. I had to finish my understanding of the true meaning of suffering. When you can relate to another soul who has suffered in extreme then you can help them heal. This realization began my healing.

God had told me I would have pain when I returned to my body. However, in the moment when you are asked to be a part of something so divine, so much bigger than anything that you have ever been a part of or experienced, that knowledge you were given in regards to the pain just slips right past your mind.

Over there at that moment, I was not feeling anything physical. There was no pain from the lightning, only an ethereal sense of love. It was only afterward, when I came back into my body that I understood and remembered what He had said about there being pain. The pain, now back in my body, was nearly my ultimate undoing. My mind went numb to it for quite some time. I think that was the only way for me to adjust to it and the new memories I was experiencing. I now coexist with the pain that was given to me, as well as the knowledge that I returned with. My lightning trip over to the other side and my God trip back has taught me so much compassion for others. It has given me a new sense of self-purpose and understanding. Everything we encounter and survive is meant to teach us a lesson. What we learn from those lessons is ultimately what we will use to save the lives of others in need.

My pain is not gone. I still carry it as my reminder as to why I am still here. Let's just say I have now found my own new sense of self, a new balance of healing in my physical body. It is the best that I could hope for. As for my emotional healing, I have balanced that too. The mental? Well, I didn't have a mental problem after all. I was just hit by a couple bolts of lightning. If I am missing a few puzzle pieces, I have no more worries. I am just painting my new self a new picture!

~~~

My intuition knows that I am the dot

that connects me to my everything.

All I have to do is listen.

~8~

BOND

Thoughts of you
Bring silly emotions
Laughter so deep
Never know where it's going
I can't even tell you
How I survive a day without you
All I do know
Is distance means nothing
You get me
Like a mirror image of myself
We always know
What the other is saying
No explanation needed
As the tears start rolling
As we laugh so hard
We can't seem to speak
I cherish every one
Of those memories
They have to last forever
Just in case
Life gets too busy
For us to find the time

For me this poem represents my sisters. I also have a few very close friends that this sister bond has happened with. There are no rules as to being blood-related. As long as you've experienced that, laugh yourself silly, finish each other's sentences, shoot water out your nose, and that kind of thing, then you know exactly what I am talking about. You have felt the bond!

For those of you who love your sisters, celebrate! For those of you who don't, I'm truly sorry. I hope you have found some friends to fill that gap. I have tried to live without mine and I find it impossible. Nothing and no one gets my silly sense of humor like my sisters. Therefore, I make my time on the phone with them a priority. They are a piece of my mother. We are the last direct pieces of her. So we are there for each other, even though the miles separate us.

Have you ever said something you thought was so hilarious, but nobody else laughed? This happens to me all the time. When Mother got sick and we three girls were back together I realized, it's not that I'm not funny, it's that people just didn't get me. After years of being separated, the three of us picked up as if it were yesterday. We laughed at things no one else got. We practically rolled on the floor and laughed deeply with tears rolling down our cheeks! I loved those moments to see the tears roll down Mom's face right along with us as we carried on. She may or may not have gotten it, but she couldn't help it, she laughed with us. My stomach has never hurt so bad. Just think, we might not need so many sit ups if we were to make time for daily laughter sessions with our sisters!

I encourage you to find the time for deep healing laughter. Whether it be with family or friends, it is so healing to laugh. I have gone days and weeks through my tragedy without any laughter. I did not even realize how much our body and mind could be fed by this simple expression. It has an amazing effect on our mental outlook on life. We need only to re-experience it once before our brains become hungry for it and crave that feeling more often. Allow yourself to feel the abundance of deep healing laughter.

My sisters and I were very close in our youth. As teenagers we started moving on in life away from each other. Each of us went in our own direction, different states, jobs, and raising our own families. We would talk on the phone and keep up with all the normal transitions of life, but when our mom got sick it was as if she knew something that we didn't. She relocated to be closer to me, just months before her diagnosis. By doing this, she had made a halfway point for both my sisters to come and stay. This is what brought us back together and what healed all of our lost time with each other.

I know how easy it is to let time get away from you in your daily routines, but take from this experience. Make the time to be close with your family. Laugh, play, sled, ice skate, dress up for Halloween, do puzzles, tell silly stories, make glitter pictures, tape on a fake mustache, and wear an eye patch! Just spend quality time together, while you have the chance, and please, make sure you laugh! When you total up the four months of time that we shared with our mother before she passed over, we laughed more than we cried.

~~~

~ Post a sticky note on your bathroom mirror ~

I am extraordinary.

I am loved.

I am worth every blessing

that my creator has bestowed

upon me.

Baby, you are a beautiful being!

~ Repeat this to yourself often! ~

~9~

FALL

The leaves
Are changing color
The air
Has a new scent
Autumn's crisp chill
Dances over my skin
The passing of time
A new season begins
As the leaves
Do their dance
I sit and I watch
Floating, spiraling
My thoughts
Become lost
The tree is left standing
Naked and bare
For the first time
I notice
Its pure
Uncovered beauty
The roots
The trunk
The textured skin bark
The solidity and strength
And then I see
Branches
Reaching toward heaven
As if offering
Wide open arms
To anyone
Who is in need

Fall was my mother's favorite season. I hardly took the time to notice. To me it meant one season closer to winter and a long stretch of cold. Cold is not a friend to my body. After my encounter with lightning, I was left with blood vessels that were to damaged to feed my feet properly. I had to have nine toes amputated due to inadequate blood flow. Also, my left ankle needed reconstructed due to the stretching of tendons from the initial injury which had left me very unstable to walk. As the cold weather approaches I have less feeling in my extremities and I am left with a much deeper, more excruciating pain. It is hard to explain and even harder to understand, but I have severe nerve damage and neuropathy in my extremities. It has created an interesting pattern of seasonal challenges for me to overcome every year.

I see trees as amazing structures that fascinate me and I have figured out why I love them so much. I relate to the trees because they represent the roots, the foundation, the trunk, as well as the core and growth, just as I see my body and spirit. I would never have realized how much I connect to the beauty of those big, beautiful trees if I had not stared at them from summer, to fall, and into winter. Just passing the time, thinking of my mother and her life, I watched the transition before my eyes. It felt like slow motion as the leaves went from their blooming lustrous fullness to a fading of hot fall color, and in the end, bare. Four months of time had passed right in front of my eyes. Since it had become a pastime for my sisters and I, it was no wonder we all connected these changes that were bringing us closer to our mothers time left here on Earth.

For me, the trees began to symbolize an immense amount of strength I was seeing in three young women who were on a journey to find God's meaning in our devastating circumstance. I began to relate to the structure of the bare trees in so many ways. From the powerful hit of a lightning bolt, to the storms we have to weather in life. Some create a dismayed wonder as if to say, "How am I still standing here?" Our bodies shed our skin, just as the tree sheds its leaves. Our trunks keep us standing and our roots are only as deep as we want or need them to be. We can be as strong as an old oak tree or as whimsical as a willow, but we all have strength. The changes that take place in life are the lessons we each need for our own personal growth.

When you feel as though life is putting to much upon your shoulders, dig into the soil with your roots, hold on with all the strength you have inside your trunk, and learn to let your arms bend with the wind. Flexibility is key to keeping yourself standing through any and every storm that may pass through your life. Without being flexible you would crack apart in the first storm that crossed over your path. Our lives can mirror the image of the tree if you only take the time to see the connection. Look at the scars, see what the tree has survived, and realize that you too can be that strong. Lift your arms to heaven, gather your strength, and share your knowledge and experience with any one who is in need. You may never know that the person you were too shy to speak to may have needed your message for hope, for direction, and to realize that they have a purpose in this life. Be strong and don't miss your opportunity to stand tall and majestic.

Resistance to change

may hold you back from

your meant to be moment in life.

Embrace new beginnings and

allow your spirit to thrive.

~10~

DOORS

As I look in your eyes
I see the light to your soul
A need to move forward
Fearing the unknown
The door stands wide open
Life waiting
For you to go
Do not be afraid
I want you to know
Life is full of uncertainty
A mystery of unknowns
A landslide of emotion
So just let it flow
Intuition is trying to guide you
Down the path
You need to go
So when that new door opens
It is time
For the old one
To close

I know so many people who won't allow themselves to let go of the past. When the current experience is finished, you should not still be holding onto the door behind you while your other hand is holding onto the next door in front of you. You have to make a conscious decision to close one so that you may walk into your next life lesson, the next experience of your life, with an open heart and mind. However, you do bring the lessons and knowledge from your past with you into your next experience. That lesson is a reminder, a memory, a piece of your puzzle. It is meant to help you recognize, not to repeat, the same lessons over and over. Finish up the experience you are standing in, review what you have learned, and consciously envision yourself closing the door behind you. Allow yourself to move forward with the memories and lessons, not the baggage which should be left behind. You do not need the burden of that baggage to weigh you down or hold you back from your forward progression. Gather the pieces of your life and put the picture puzzle together as you want it to look. The picture that is left behind when your life is over is the picture that others will see of how you lived your life. It is a picture of you and your legacy, the inspiration of the person that others will aspire to be.

When you open your mind to change, the changes will start happening for you. It is generally fear of change that holds us back or fear of the unknown in front of us. When you allow that fear to become a part of your everyday life, your forward experiences stop. It is then time to ask yourself, what are you afraid of? Make the list of fears, really allow yourself to analyze them. You will probably find there are really not as many things to be afraid of because it really is just doubt inside you. Your self-esteem is in need of a boost. If you have lived in this cycle for a long period of time you probably aren't even aware of how low your confidence level really has become. This lesson of writing these things down will help you distinguish between the fears and doubts. Make a few columns on your paper and start crossing off the small fears and turn the doubts into goals to build your self-esteem. Pick a few things you are really good at and start to focus on them. A little bit at a time works better than doing everything all at once. It will be a transition in your mind to believe in yourself. When you believe, you become more positive.

I want to touch on the fact that not everybody will support the positive changes in you. Sometimes we surround ourselves with people who are already comfortable with the way you were before. That being said, it may be that those people are part of the reason of why you became fearful and full of doubt. If those around you truly love and support you, they will support the positive changes you are trying to make. I am not living in your life, so I do not know the choice of your surroundings. I have been a part of helping people heal through many different situations, and this one seems to be the most common.

Ultimately, the choice is up to you. If you want to change your life into what you feel you were meant to be doing, then you will make that choice. There will be no one who can hold you back once you set your mind to it. Being able to gather the tools to recognize that it is not very difficult will help you have less fear of your unknown.

It turns into a decision deep inside that knows when the day is right for you to make a change. Your new door is standing in front of you. As you turn around and close the one behind you, lock it and walk into the new you.

~~~

Life is too short

to waste your time

holding onto the wrong door.

If you feel the need

to hold doors open.

Try holding them open

out of kindness

for others.

~11~

CONNECTION

Music and lyrics
The answers are found
A peace that is needed
To stand on solid ground
The music calms anxiety
The lyrics touch the soul
They together
Balance me so
That I can see clearly
Know where I need to go
Life experiences of the writer
Soothing voice of the singer
Heartbeat of the drummer
Mingling mix of the bass
Magical dance of the guitar
You can become one with the song
It balances mind and spirit
A feeling of connection
That someone has felt
The same as I
Healing takes over
A knowing
That in this creation of sound
A connection can be found

In the process of my recovery I found my biggest healing moments through music. The lyrics connected the memories of my forgotten past. A drum beat could calm my erratically racing, beating out of sync, rhythmically dysfunctional, out of control heart. Believe me, my heart was not in good communication with my brain, nor was my brain with the rest of my body. They did what they wanted, when they wanted. Focusing on the music and lyrics was the best medicine I had found. The guitar and bass could carry my emotions to a place where my pain could be controlled. The voice of the singer would transport my ailing body and spirit to another plane. I could relax and be soothed into a hypnotic state of mind to gain control over the malfunctions of my brain and the lack of communication to the rest of my body. Through all the trauma to my body and mind I do not think I could have gained the control that was needed to overcome the pain of my ailments had I not had the music.

Music is amazing. It can help heal you if you learn to relax and listen. It allows you to fit in, even when you are different. Music has no boundaries of race, language, or financial status. It is just you and the song. We can each find something we connect with individually. The beauty of it is each person's ability to relate, interpret, and take from it, the connection that feels right for you. The lyrics tell a story, but the connection of that story is open to each interpretation: it allows you to find your own parallel to your own life experiences.

I have been around people in the music industry and have had the knowledge of what a particular song may have been written about. It is never a surprise to me to hear a person tell their story to one of the band members. They will explain what a song has done for them and how a particular song has saved their life. They will describe how they have turned things around because of the words that they were able to feel, as though the song was written to them personally. Some have changed a tragic situation into something they can now survive, whereas before the song they had no direction and no idea how they would get through. The music, the lyrics, and the creation of one song made it possible for them to see better days ahead. Music is like magic that way. We all hear it differently, relate to it in our own way, and find the meant to be connection for each of us. Even if the written song had absolutely nothing to do with the experience you are comparing it to, it was still meant for you to hear it. Music is, and will always be, a centering balance for your body and soul. Just like art it will always be open for each individual person's own interpretation.

That is why music became my meditation. It allowed me to relax into a place and start a chain reaction into my new beginnings. Music became my divine intervention. It was the one thing that connected my broken memories from my past to the new healing power put around me after my encounter with lightning. I, too will admit to knowing a few songs in particular that have saved my shattered life and put me back on the road of living. I have personally shared my story with one person who wrote the song that saved me. As it turns out, the real meaning of the song had nothing to do with what I had related it to. And so, know that the universe works in mysterious ways. It was still what I needed to hear at the exact moment that I needed to start living again.

~~~

Karma can bite you

When you least expect it

Regrets are always hard to swallow

When one realizes

That kindness should always rule

Do not be left

Standing on the sidelines

Looking like a lonely fool

~12~

BELIEVE

As parents
We are protective
As society
We are judgmental
Is it so wrong to encourage
A child
To become their passion
Truly allow them
To be who they are
Give them the tools
To live it
Allow them the desire
To breathe it in
Let the journey of learning it
Flow over them
Like the wind
Experience all
That life has to offer
Never once thinking
Those words
I can't
To see the world
As a blank piece of paper
Theirs to create
Always knowing
That you understand

As parents I believe the greatest gift we can offer our children is to encourage a child to live life through their passion. I have encouraged my children to find an interest and see if it suits them. Is it something that can fulfill a dream, a desire, a driving need inside of them? Does it give a deep sense of self-gratification? Would it change the world, or simply make it a better place? Make them feel fed and nourished inside since they have such passion for what they have chosen. I would rather them be happy in this journey of self-growth than to be wasting their time, just doing something to get by. An individual's journey of employed work is a very long road. As society becomes more frustrated with the lack of kindness given to them by so many employees in the retail businesses, our customer service skills are lacking. We have forgotten to be compassionate and caring in our society. The local clerk, the person on the phone, the nurse in a hospital, your misery shows! If you do not find some sort of happiness in your chosen profession, change it! If only each of us were encouraged to become something we have a passion for or were given the opportunity to choose who we really want to be simply because we love it, our world would be a much happier place.

I have seen teachers encourage only a college degree path. When the student veers away from that choice, they are pushed to military or law enforcement as if no other careers are acceptable in our society. What about the arts? What about the trades? We still need people to build things! We are losing our creativity to allow our world to be a better place. What about asking them what they truly desire? I worked in many different areas trying to find what and who I wanted to be. The only thing that I knew for sure is that I wanted to make a difference in the lives of others. I have slimed fish in Alaska, worked the fishing boats, laid electrical lines, built snow roofs, waited tables, worked for the airlines, made cedar boxes for a place that made handblown glass out of Mt. St. Helen's ash, and I joined the Army.

My entire life experiences were spent searching for my meant to be purpose. Had I been encouraged to be passionate for what I was meant to be while here on this orbital globe I would have written the books years ago! God has given each of us a gift with a purpose and society tries to mold us into pieces of clay to fit our decorative surroundings. Look around, God created each one of us beautiful and different, each in our own way. Each of us created in the image of Him. Why are we forgetting that? He never intended us to all be molded into the same piece of clay!

I hear parents encouraging their children when they are young, but when the teen years appear the parent tries to change the rules. It is no longer encouragement to live your dream or find God's meant to be purpose for you, but to complete college and get a degree and get a good job. A good job should be doing something you love so much that you make every person you cross paths with feel thankful they were blessed to meet you that day. We have only so much time to make our lessons count. Make use of your time to fulfill your life's journey. Leave nothing undone. Encourage your children to live their passion. While you're at it, find your passion too.

~~~

I'll hold your hand

Until you find your place

When you decide to let go

It will not erase

My connection to you

Or the bond

That we share

I am your Mom

I will always be there

Wherever you travel

No matter how far

The life you have chosen

Will carry you far

You live in your passion

You're never alone

My heart will always

Be connected to yours

~13~

FEAR

Fear of dying
Creates fear of living
One controls the outcome of the other
So I'll help you understand
To fear death
Holds you back
From the meant to be
Experience of life
Not living
Keeps you away from the journey
The path that is yours
Chosen by you
When you choose to fear death
Your forward progression slows
When you choose living over fear
You walk in the knowing of meant to be
Your soul will recognize
The power of your existence
Your mind makes the connection
Then body follows suit
A balance is created
As fear becomes replaced
By living

I know I am repeating myself here, but live your passion! Live your dream! Live your meant to be moments in life! I can't stress this enough, if you get nothing more out of this book, get this! Death is inevitable. For every single one of us. It is one of your meant to be moments in life. Do not waste your time and energy on fearing this. Fear is wasting your living, and your time is passing by without you. Find a balance in your existence to complete your purpose for being. God granted you an existence to live, to make your choices, to find the meaning of you, to fulfill the growth experience of your soul. Find what defines your spiritual existence. We each are gifted with something special inside of us. Something that sets us apart from every other soul in human form. God knows what that special part of you is. It's up to you to find it and make something extraordinary out of it.

Try something new, eat something different, travel to a place you have never been. Meet new people, listen to a new kind of music, ride a bike, have a picnic in the rain. Do something! Get out of your fear zone. Make a list of things that you are to afraid to try and then do them!

Truly walking on your path is knowing that the universe will help open new doors to you so that you are able to walk in your light of living. Let this be your moment of divine intervention. Know that there is nothing ordinary about you. Know that the only person that matters in your life already believes in you! He made you who you are! He has no doubts about the lessons that you are meant to learn. When our days come to an end, and they will end, I don't want you to have regrets for all the things that you wish you would have at least attempted.

Although there may be times when you feel alone, like you are only a dot in this world and nobody sees that you are not living, you are wrong! I died and I stood on the other side of the veil of light that separates our existence. I know that God sees all and feels all. He can feel the pain and fear you are living in right now. He lives through us and our living of life's experiences. Do not define yourself by the lack of your living. Redefine the true you by being the seeker of your meant to be you. Kick your fear to the curb and remind yourself that you are not alone. Now, get yourself out there and start living!

~~~

Doubt less ~ Believe more

Think less ~ Dream more

Regret less ~ Choose more

Follow less ~ Become more

Cry less ~ Laugh more

Wait less ~ Achieve more

Rest less ~ Live more

Hate less ~ Love more

Stress less ~ Create more

As you learn to believe in the dream you have chosen, you will see that the picture of who you have become laughs more often, achieves the goals which have been started, and is now living the life you have always wanted. You are loving the person you have created.

~14~

TIME

Time passes
Creates yesterdays
Did I live that day
For all it was worth
Not waste a moment
On doubt without words
My self-expression
Of creative mind
Is what will
Be left behind
As I near the end
Of my life
Of my time
So today I will write
The words that will guide
Another who questions
The passing of time

This life is a journey, a choice of paths you choose to take. Each one leading you to a new adventure, a new direction, and a new destination. How long it takes, how hard or how easy it will be, is all a choice of growth to you and your soul. If you choose to gain the knowledge of the lesson quickly, you can move on. Should you choose to refuse to see that you are in control of your choices, then you may allow yourself a very long and terribly hard path. This path ultimately will still lead you back to making a choice, a decision, and a change. The factor of time spent on the path and the lesson is up to you. Time becomes the ultimate factor on our journeys. We all have a tendency to waste so much of it. Take me, for instance. I knew I was going to write these books ever since I was 18 years old. However, I spent the next twenty plus years experiencing life, my paths, those meant to be experiences on my journey. Not in the sense that time was wasting, but in the element of what I was meant to learn. Now I have completed those lessons and I am able to share with you the information I have gathered, the tools needed for certain situations, and the method of healing it takes to survive some of the most unbearable situations that we are faced with on our paths.

Living life to the best of your soul's ability is not as easy as it would seem when we are young and unafraid. Youth has a way of allowing us to feel the invincibility of ourselves. We have no fear of living, experiencing everything possible, and loving to the greatest depths. Until one day, we get hurt. Pain, whether emotional or physical, can derail our limitless dreams. Pain creates the inhibitions inside our hearts and minds. It can stop our forward motion, our progression, and our life as we are meant to be living it. That's how it seems as we are standing in the emotion and feeling the pain. How long you stand in it is up to you. Take a moment to step outside your emotional involvement in it and pretend to see it through a window. Once you detach yourself from the emotion you are often able to view it more clearly. Then you are more able to move forward out of the situation. You then see that crossroad on your path. Your choice becomes more evident and much easier for you to finally choose. The choice of that timing is up to you.

I can only show you how to look at your life and time, finding your path is a choice for you. I can give you some examples to choose from but, like a multiple choice question, we all have a choice to the right answer for us. Expecting someone else to fix you or make your life change only leads you back to your personal responsibility to choose what is best for you and your soul purpose before you run out of time.

~~~

You are never too old

to change the direction

of your dream.

You are never to young to become

who you know you are meant to be.

Age has nothing to do with the path

you knew you were meant to walk.

It is the second hand just ticking by.

Can you hear it say,

"tick-tock?"

~15~

DOTS

Life scatters abroad
Like a dot to dot
A picture that's unfolding
That I can see not
We seem to feel invincible
Some battles not yet fought
A landscape of experience
Lessons we've been taught
Learning this and that
Not giving it a thought
Never knowing
That the connections in life
Is what is being sought
When you open up your book of life
To see what you have brought
Do not be surprised to see
You have connected
Your dot to dot

When we try to remember our lives, back to our earliest memories, a picture begins to paint itself. We can remember random times and moments of happiness, tragedy, sadness, holidays, school, movies, and music. Now try to look at your life from today, at this moment, backwards. Put into place a dot on each of the memories that have affected the today you. What dots made you who you are today? What dots define you and the character of who you have become? What lessons fed your soul to the point of knowing that you were doing exactly what you were put on this Earth to do; who you were meant to be. Are you that person? Have there been times of regret for not fulfilling something you know you felt a burning need inside to accomplish. Did you get scared or did it become too hard for you to complete the task? It is never too late to return to your dot picture and redefine the true person you were meant to be. When your days are over and you look at the life journey you lived, I want you to be satisfied with the person you were. Don't wait until an ending to try to apologize to those you love or feel you have let down. You are responsible for only you. If you lack something you should have completed during your existence, regain it now. Allow yourself to try again. Repair what you are unsatisfied with. Recreate the picture of you and your life. If your life was too difficult at times and you walked away and left a piece of your soul behind you, go back. Make amends, retrieve those parts of you. You are stronger now and have the ability to reconcile the past mistakes of your journey. That is part of your lesson here. Remember, you have a purpose of existence. Once you gather your missing pieces, you can move into being the strong amazing soul you were meant to be.

When I died, I was greeted by three elders, who were in charge of my book of life. They showed me my dots, my pictures, and my experiences all unfolding into a story of my lifetime thus far. I was able to see the ups, downs, and meant to be moments in my life story. I was shown this so that when I came back I would bring awareness to others about the time we are wasting for our soul's growth. It was important for me to understand this path of choices that we each have. With each outcome being the effect of the choice that was made. It made me exceptionally aware of my responsibility in the lives of others, as they connect to the paths that I choose. Now I will weigh my choices out with more thought. Each path I take will have a different affect on my soul's growth and experience, knowing that they connect the dots of my life and yours.

If you find that you are already in the beautiful place of happiness, satisfaction, and glorious life completion, then celebrate you! When you look at your dotted picture, it should reflect the person that you have become, a souls journey completed and a life learned as well as it could be learned.

Now, go ahead and color it inside or outside the lines. The choice is yours!

~~~

Never say never

Life has a way of showing you

That never always has a possibility

We will often manifest to life

Those things we try to push

The farthest away

~16~

CHOICES

We love we laugh
We live our lives
Through the ones
We've touched in life
In each and every
Place unknown
Sharing knowledge
As we go
Our choices by chance
Can bring consequence
Try to do well
To teach to guide
Show others a way
To succeed in life
Not stress and doubt
Nor try to hide
Some lessons are tough
The outcome a must
For your soul to grow
And live in the knowing
That each lesson completed
You were never defeated

It is a necessity on my journey to help a person feel better than they did a moment ago. If I cross your path, it is never by chance. I made a conscious choice to be a better person. Not better than anyone else, but better than I have to be, for the purpose and growth of my soul. I am aware of the energy of others around me. I pay attention to what I feel a person needs. The value we place in helping others for no gain comes back to you regardless. If you treat people badly, that comes back around too. I do believe in karma. I also believe what goes around, comes back around, for the good as well. One random moment of kindness could save a person's life! That fact alone makes me be the kind person I know I was placed on this Earth to be. I can also be tough on people, when I am coaching or teaching or guiding another, on how to break the bad patterns of their paths. Believe me, when I have said the same thing 444 times, in every different way I can say it, I get tough. Some have feared it as me being mean. I am not a mean person! I just don't like drama or procrastination. I have only so much of me to share with each person with whom I cross paths. Only so much time on my own journey that sometimes I feel as though my time is not appreciated. There is always another person who would love to have one-on-one time with me. If a person has agreed to help you through your most difficult lessons, take it seriously. Dedicate yourself to you and the person who has been placed in your life to help lift you back on your feet. There is a very real possibility that Angels do walk this Earth, some living their own life lessons, even as they are helping you with yours. You never know who will appear to help you on your journey. Make it a priority to become a better you. If you are being given that chance, make sure you appreciate the choices as well.

Do not allow yourself to become defeated by the choices you made which created the circumstances of the experience you are standing in at this very moment. You, and only you, can make your life take a turn to walk a better road. Get out your personal journal, tablet, or sticky pad and start writing the great qualities about yourself. This is not a project to feel boastful, but rather to see that you have qualities in you you need to recognize. Draw a line down the middle and make a list of your not so good qualities. Be honest! This is not a test and is meant to give you a tool to see the balance of who you are. Next, turn your paper over. Write down the goals you have to achieve to help you be the person that you would rather be. Finding the root of you, the good, the bad, and the future you, is a visual tool. It can give you a true clearer picture, like looking through the window outside of the emotion. Acknowledging that you are not perfect and have work to do on yourself is key to being successful. As you start achieving those goals and becoming a better person, you will move your accomplishments to the quality side of your list. This will help you see the progress you are making. It really is very simple; don't make it complicated. Fix the broken parts of you, one piece at a time, with baby steps if you need. This journey is also not a race to the finish line, but a journey to become the best you possible.

~~~

Life choices

can be compared to choosing

the right flavor

of a simple little jellybean...

Do not make it complicated.

Just choose...

The one you most desire.

~17~

KNOWING

I don't want
Your heart to be heavy
I already know
Where my soul is meant to go
Doubt shares a space
That is occupied by many
I'm just not allowed
To walk down
That road
No matter what
I will always love you
Regardless
For we each have a journey
Of lessons to learn
We can't put a price
On the path to help others
It is a sacrifice in life
That could cost us the most
Failure to me
Isn't even an option
For my existence alone
Could have already been done
Perseverance and kindness
Always sharing my guidance
Healing through compassion
Is what He sent back with me
To carry on

When you know from the deepest places inside your own soul that you are meant to do something amazing on this planet and that the universe has opened a door for you to walk through, let nothing stop you! We have become a society of bad listeners due to not listening to our own intuition, gut feelings, or the burning desires can carry us to our greatest success. Instead, we look to others for confirmation on what they think we should be doing. What are their opinions of our ideas? How do they think the plan will unfold? When we don't get crowned with ecstatic excitement over our amazing ideas, or hear the answer we felt we knew inside of us, we allow the advice or opinion of another to make us doubt our ideas and meant to be moments. We give our crowns away! We doubt what we thought was the greatest thing to ever pass through our minds, hearts, and through our souls. Why? It was never the other person's destiny or dream. Why would they think our idea was the right way of doing something? You must learn to listen! God gave you those instincts to know what is right for you, how best to protect yourself from the doubts and negativity of others. So listen to yourself, to your intuition, your very own gut instinct. Do not seek the opinions of others for clarification to your own destiny.

It is your dream! Your path! Your journey! Your meant to be! Embrace the future that has been planned for you. Write the story of your own book, your book of life!

Start surrounding yourself with those who want to see you succeed. If you aren't able to find them in the beginning, don't give up. Eventually you will attract them to you, ones that are meant to be in your circle or space. Will will attract the support team needed to believe in your dream. When you are walking the path that you are meant to be walking, doubt cannot penetrate the bubble of protection placed around you. There may be butterflies in the pit of your stomach, but not doubt. Stand up, fix your crown, and get moving. There is no better time than today to start living for your soul's purpose.

When I was young, I knew something deep inside about myself. I was never encouraged to be who I knew I could be, or any of the things that I teach my children, but I knew. For every horrible, negative thing said to me, I felt a whisper of knowledge that those things being said weren't true. For every beating I took to my defenseless body, I felt a strength of someone invisible trying to protect me from believing that I was worthless, as I was being told. For every moment that I was not allowed to cry through my pain, I felt an intensely positive purpose searing into my subconscious.

As time passed I was hit by the lightning. When I died, met my creator, and was given the choice to come back to help you, I knew. I knew why I needed the whisper of knowledge, the strength of the invisible, and the recognition of that burning path. I knew that I could handle the journey back through it all. God knew that I was strong enough and so did I. I knew.

Now it's time to follow what you know is your meant to be, planned out, purpose. When the path chosen is for the betterment of others, you will not fail. A true heart can create peace wherever it travels. Believe in yourself and your ability to leave this world with a legacy of faith, truth, and belief that every person's dream in life matters.

~~~

Try not to base your happiness for the future

on your unhappy experiences from the past.

We need to live and love ourselves

in the present.

Unhappiness comes from us constantly debating

the outcome of things

we have absolutely no control over.

Let go of the pain of past hurts.

Work to better improve

your thoughts for a happier you.

Today is a fabulous day to start living.

~18~

TRANSITION

As I walk my path
I will have no regrets
Every lesson I learn
With my honor intact
My heart may feel heavy
Confusion fogs my mind
New lessons cross my path
Never knowing what I'll find
I know that I am ready
To move into my next experience
Without expectation
Only acceptance
For the path I walk is sacred
My soul is guided to lead
Others on their journey
A walk into their destiny

As you begin the transition into the new awareness of you, who you are meant to be, what you are meant to be doing, and where your journey will take you next, I want you to realize the experiences that trail behind you. Look back to see the journey you have walked. Good or bad, the choices were made to bring you to where you are standing now. If what you see does not please you, make a change. A visual perspective of your past will help you shape your future. If what you see has made you into the person you have strived to become, move into the next phase of your life journey. Challenge yourself to accomplish something you have secretly desired doing or were too afraid to become. I have only acceptance for the choices that I am responsible for making. I have no expectations of others. The only expectations I allow, are for myself. It goes with the fact that you cannot change another person's actions, choices, or the way they live their lives. The only person you will ever be able to change is you. Lead others through the positive way that you live. Let them want to be better because they want it. Accept them for who they are and stay focused on your own challenges and changes in front of you. Change becomes contagious to others around you. The energy that surrounds you will be felt by them. I still have a little bit of nagging guilt that will sit upon my shoulder from time to time. I am always wanting to over help someone or turn them in a half circle and scoot them onto the path that I can see would better suit their life journey, but I have to pull myself away from what they may be refusing to see and let them make their own mistakes. Walking your right path is a transition, a journey of choices in itself so that you can see where you came from when you get to where you are meant to be.

In the vast grandeur of the universe we can say that no choice made is the wrong choice. Each soul here is learning something. Not every person will understand the choices the other is making. However, we may do well to remind ourselves that without bad, we would not know good. Without choice, we would not be able to change the bad path to something better. That is what another soul will learn from one's poor choice of experience. We have to have all kinds, even the kind who beat me as a child, so that we can choose a better existence and overcome all obstacles of the journey our souls are in need of learning.

Let me clarify: I do not condone the deplorable behavior of others. I do not think the person who beat me has changed. Nor, has he ever shown love or kindness to anyone that I know. The choice is still available to him. When his time and existence runs out, he can then account for it in his book of life. That is not on me, for I have allowed my soul to grow from the inner strength God has blessed me with. I look at it as my life lesson to make me as strong as I could possibly have been, to endure my survival of returning to this planet to help others. I am who I am because of the experiences I have survived. I simply pray that they will learn from their lessons and make a wiser choice to become a better soul. One bad choice in life can derail a person's entire existence if they refuse to see a better path. That is their choice. God has given us free will to choose. We only have to make the choice.

~~~

When you are dealing with drama,

you have the choice

to feed it or deflate it.

Turn your back on it.

Walk out of the emotion of it.

It only serves to disrupt your balance

if you choose to immerse yourself

in the negative flow

of drama.

~19~

SUNSHINE

I feel the light
Wash over me
Refuels my soul
Helps me breath
Deeply
My body takes it in
To the depths
Of my being
Helps me feel centered
Again
This light is a gift
From up above
A touch
Of pure balance
An energy within
As I feel its heat move through me
It enables me to move
Forward again

Oh the power of the sun! Refuel yourself. Bask in the energy as it penetrates to the center of your being. Books have already been written on the needs and purposes of this wonderful giant ball of hot fire but seriously, allow yourself to acknowledge its beautiful healing powers the next time you go outside. When your mind is in its own disfunction and things are out of sync, go outside, sit, and don't think. Close your eyes, place your face towards its heat, and feel the serenity penetrate into your being. The massive amount of revitalizing energy this gift from above can give to your being is amazing. It can drain away the stresses and imbalances of your day. Allow yourself five minutes to take some deep breaths in. Feel the heat as it touches your skin. Picture its rays healing, centering, and renewing your balance again.

I often relate the sun with smiling, happy people. They seem to thrive, regardless of their troubles. They have an intimate relationship with the sun. They spend a significant amount of time outdoors and seem to be much happier because of it. It leads me to the subject of the new recognition and understanding which is being brought up more frequently by our doctors: low vitamin D levels. It seems as though doctors are focusing more on this. It appears that low vitaminD levels may have connections to other things being off balance in our bodies. I recently found out that my level is low and have been addressing it. This makes sense since I do not spend a great deal of time outdoors. I also rarely use artificial forms of sunlight. Don't get me wrong, I love the outdoors, but rarely find it enjoyable to be out in the ninety degree heat. I am from The Great Northwest and still have not acclimated to high heat indices. Still, I think the doctors are on to something here. If simply increasing your vitamin D level can increase your energy level and possibly help your mood, get it checked. I do know that we as a society spend a significant amount of time indoors.

In recent years I have heard about several kinds of seasonal disorders that affect our mood cycles. Staying indoors through long winters, lengthy rain seasons, and working makes this a little easier to recognize and understand. Our bodies need sunlight just as the plants, trees, and grass growing outside. It is just my observation, but I think we need to make the time. Take five minutes just to let the sun soak into you. Since this is a book of learning, you can do something as simple as this. It could help you find a connection to your moods and it is free. A few minutes to yourself, a little meditation time, and a form of refueling your body. It doesn't get any easier than that.

~~~

Today is the day

The day that you

Give yourself a second chance

At life ~ At faith ~ At being

Who you

Were always meant to be.

~20~

SPOTLIGHT

I wish
That you
Were with me
Standing
Here today
Watching
All the fans
Scream loud
Just waiting
For us to play
Your excitement
Would've glowed
Like spotlights
Across your face
Your friends
All out there
Working
While you
Got to stand
Side stage
I know
You
Would have loved this
Standing
Proud
As only
A Dad could be
Then I feel it
In a whisper
As its essence
Embraces my being
You were standing
Right next to me

I wrote this for a friend of mine who is in the music business. He told me a story about his father and how proud it would always make him to see his son and bandmates perform. As fate would have it, he lost his father too soon in his life. It was a loss he has felt each time he has performed at a large venue or on a prestigious tour. Those were the moments when he felt most alone. To him his father missed the best, most successful parts of his career. To his father though, he now has the best seat in the house!

This is a great reminder to each of us who have experienced loss of someone dear and close to our hearts. I often cross the paths of people who have the hardest milestone of their life because of the death of somebody they loved. I too, have experienced that loss. I do understand the imbalance of emotions from this terribly emotional experience. However, since I have also experienced my own death; It gives me that extra knowledge from both sides of loss. The best message I can share with you is that they are present in your life for those big glorious performances, as well as the private moments when you are sitting home alone, missing them with all your heart. They can feel the anguish that surrounds your being. Your loved one wants nothing more than for you to find a peace inside your soul, just as they are at peace through their own passing. It is so good for you to remember them and all the things you loved so much about your person. I want to remind you that the memories do not stop when your grief is set free. Letting go of your emotional pain is not going to mean that you don't still love them as much as when they were standing beside you. You are just allowing yourself to love them in a more special way.

Remember, heaven isn't like going to jail! Your loved ones who have passed can visit you as they please! Take the time to talk to them, let them know you feel their presence. Do not be afraid when you feel their ethereal presence around you. Allow yourself to heal your sadness in honor of their ability to get through to you. For without healing it is a murky energy that surrounds your being. When you hang onto this sad energy you make it more difficult for them to let you know they are alright in their afterlife. Cleanse your emotional pain and move yourself into your spiritual light.

Once you feel balanced you may feel the essence of your loved one. You may dream of them or you may even be given a sign that they are around you. It may even feel like you are standing in the spotlight, living in your dream.

~~~

If you are going to quit something,

let it be your procrastination.

Every time you put off your dream,

you hold yourself back

from your own

meant to be.

You tell yourself

you will do it tomorrow,

As your days turn into weeks,

your weeks turn into months,

your months turn into years,

you look back and realize,

that your tomorrow

has turned into

your never.

~21~

YOU

I am so happy
To be alive
Don't like to imagine
What I would have missed
If I hadn't survived
For most
Life is a mystery
As well as death
I can only describe
The energy the love the book
The ultimate choice
Of the road that I took
So my friend I tell you
Just take a good look
At the choices you make
The path that you walk
Your life journey
Is a plan with a plot
To bring you full circle
With the ones who are sought
To help close a door
Or open a new thought
Do not be afraid
Or question too long
For you had a hand in planning
The rights and the wrongs
I'll cross your path to help
Give you strength
And guide you through
Help to close a few doors
And open up some new
Build your strength back up again
So your vision sees right through
Your brand new meaning
Your existence, you

I will be forever grateful for the choice God gave to me. That single moment; within a flash in time, I was standing on the other side in my afterlife to be given an ultimate, selfless, and life changing choice. To come back to this life. To do what I was destined to do. To be who I was chosen to be. To show people how to have the ultimate faith in their destinies.

I loved my time on the other side so much that I wanted to cross over completely. I was told that I could stay over there where I was, safe and free. I would have stayed, but for that one moment when The universe decided to play an interception of my life and death path, it changed my mind and my way of living forever. I was told by God that He had work for me to do. He needed me to show others the faith and strength to survive their living. There was a destiny for me, a plan in place for me to help those souls who no longer believed they had another choice. The ones who were losing hope, strength, and their ability to walk on blind faith. He believed in me! He believed I had what it was going to take to be open minded to people's pain and suffering without judging and characterizing all who had made mistakes. After all, I had just viewed my book. We all knew what I had already overcome and survived. I could help show people their free will of choice to change their paths before it was too late for them to do so. Show other souls that it was not impossible to make a difference. Show new meaning to each person's journey. Show people how to quit wasting their time. All I can tell you is this: when the Great Spirit asks you to help and He knows that you can make that difference in the lives of others, well, there is no other answer for me. "Yes," flew out of my mind immediately.

It took me a while to dedicate the remainder of my life journey to the betterment of humankind. I questioned my experience for about a day. I knew that something extraordinary had happened to me, but I first had to learn how to walk confidently through my own life before I could confidently teach other people how to do it in theirs. When I say walk, I mean walk without falling over due to losing nine of my toes. There is nothing to help you walk gracefully with just a baby toe on one foot, however, I can still polish it up and wear a toe ring. Bling!

Surviving everything that I had to live through after my return became a game of wonder in my mind. I wondered how I was ever going to be well enough to do it. When I finally decided I would, because I said I would, things just started falling into place. I knew that every time I shared my story with a stranger they left feeling changed. I was told countless times that I should write a book. People saw something, felt it, and were inspired by what I had to share. I think my perseverance began to overrule my doubt most of the time. The one thing I had going in my favor was that I knew what I was meant to do. I remembered why I came back. I set a course to show people the many forms of raw beauty and greatness in themselves. I wanted people to love the life they had been given and make the choice to have it be encompassing, surrounding them in the spiritual light of their meant to be. To know that their life matters. To save the lives of those who had not enough faith, teach them to believe that they could survive their journey. I became committed to show others how to live by example and through the best characteristics in life I could commit to. Truth, generosity, self-reliance, self-worth, true blind faith, passion for living, unconditional love, gratitude, love of life, and destiny. After all, we all have a destiny to remind others that the human clock ticks by each day. There is nothing to fear about dying. If you are going to fear anything, it should be the fear of not living.

That is why I am so happy to be alive. So that I could help you envision and see through that brand new meaning of your existence, your life, and you!

~~~

I would like to make it very clear that you do not need a near death experience to gather these tools. We are all on a course of life learning, life altering, and redefining who we are and who we desire to become. I don't want you to not try to make the needed changes in your own life by comparison to mine. This is a walk, together, to become a happier, stronger, more defined, and more courageous person. I only want you to find and take what feels right for you.

Enjoy the Journey

~22~

SIMPLICITY

I am but a simple soul
Helping others as I go
Finding solutions
Creating a flow
Clearing out the weakness
Feeding your growth
The message that I bring you
Walks you into the know
Changes your existence
Your burdens you let go
Like unhooking your cart of troubles
On the side of the road
Direction becomes clearer
As you lighten up your load
Then you start to listen
To the inner voice within
Your purpose in life is calling
When will you begin

Some of the most asked questions from people I have helped are: What am I supposed to be doing? What is my purpose in life? How can I help people in my lifetime? What am I doing wrong? How do you stay so positive through all that you have been through?

Nothing and everything. True blind faith. That is what I rely on each day when I open my eyes. I just flat out believe that I am doing exactly what I am supposed to be doing today. I know that the ones that I am meant to help will be placed on my path. I know that I am not allowed to judge anyone else around me, but to teach and guide. I am here to place the options in front of you and allow you the choice. I can show you the map, but where you choose to go is up to you. I try to help simplify the overwhelming need to run circles around the dilemma you may be standing in and help you see it in a simpler form and from a different view. We as humans tend to make those situations we are destined to experience as complicated and as overwhelming as we can. Why? Do you not see that you create your own dysfunction? We make our lives so difficult that some people can hardly make their own decisions anymore without another person telling them what to do and how to do it! I am only able to help, not do it for you. I can present you with the options and help you narrow down your choices, but it is not my place to live your life for you. I am not allowed to take you off of your path. I can help you find the alternative options for a less stressful journey. Awareness is the key, for once the light is turned on inside your mind, you will be able to see things more clearly. It's as simple as that.

Success starts with baby steps. If you try to run the marathon before you have walked around the block, chances are you will talk yourself out of finishing the race, probably before you even start. It is up to you to find something you have a passion for. This will help keep you interested in what you are pursuing. From there imagine yourself doing it. Close your eyes and really see it. Let yourself embrace the emotion of it. Truly allow it to encompass your being. Visualize it. If you allow yourself to get to know whatever it is you are dreaming of, you will recognize the essence of it. You will know it is right for you when its energy crosses your path. Never allow the odds that may be against you keep you from pursuing what you know and feel you were meant to do. If it is something worth doing it is worth doing as well as you possibly can. Allow yourself to be happy and appreciate what you have around you while you are working toward the essence of what you want your life to become. It really is difficult to pursue the positive in your life, especially when you are swimming in circles of negative thoughts you have created from your own doubt. It is time to let those doubts be released from your mind. Give yourself permission to seek out what you know you are trying to find.

Your purpose in this life is only waiting for you to begin. Now go make a difference and pursue your passion! The beginning of your story begins within you.

~~~

Take baby steps

Change does not happen overnight

Let go of past hurts

Look at them as stepping stones.

You wouldn't be who you are today

Without those experiences.

Find the lesson in each experience

One baby step at a time

~23~

SELFISH

No one person has the right
To cross boundaries of another
Nor impose fear or fright
Take control of anothers emotions
Make them give up the fight
To devour ones self-confidence
You know when it's not right
A master of disguise
An injustice of my rights
You take from me
My faith in humanity
As I watch so many
Turn their heads at first sight
Whether a hateful word thrown at me
A fist with contact that I did not see
As disgusting as you are
It only further saddens me
To know that what you do to others
Can only make you feel better
So that you can stand up
Shove your weight around
You are nothing to me
Just another disrespectful
Selfish bully

Abuse destroys, or it can, but only if you allow it. My youth was something that is still difficult for me to revisit. From severe abusive violence against us as children or the insanity of being a child who spent countless hours trying to understand it, nothing about it makes any sense to my mind. It always makes my heart hurt the most to converse with those who have gone through it or still are experiencing it. My head just wants to scream, run! You can make it, you do not have to be a victim! I can teach you to be a survivor, just run, now!

Abuse, whether it is physical, mental, emotional, or verbal can fracture a person's self-esteem. It can penetrate the core existence of who you are and leave you lost and broken. It has no boundaries of who it can affect. If you were born into it or you entered a relationship that has abuse, it is wrong. Your healing journey can only begin when you choose to remove yourself from your abusive situation. I will never tell you that it will be easy, it's not. The less time you stay in your situation, the sooner you will recognize what it was doing to you. It depends on the level of your abuse and the amount of time that you have had to survive within it. I won't wrap it up with a pretty bow on top and give you false hope that it will be easy to overcome. The truth is, it could take you years, but you have to start sometime. It may as well be now. Just don't give up. You are worth it. You may never be able to understand the why of what has happened to you because your brain is not prone to violent tendencies, but you can learn to understand the lessons you have learned from the experience. Ultimately, you will be a much stronger person once you allow the understanding and awareness to sink in.

I did not allow it to define me. It is part of my past and I am who I am today because it was a part of my learning path to help others. My defiance in being victimized started at a young age because I knew it was wrong. I was just too small to really fight back. Oh, how I wanted to be a bigger person so that I could defend myself and my siblings from the wrath of a bullying monster. I could never understand why he hated us so much. I stopped trying to figure that out long ago. There is no logical reason for that violent behavior. My mind will never be capable of relating to someone who is so different from me. I have positivity and light. He has negativity and darkness. I do not feed into the reasons for his behavior, I feed only the positive person I became in spite of him. I became a survivor and that has helped me survive everything I have been faced with thus far on my journey. My scars still remain, some on the surface, some on the inside. They serve as a reminder of where and what I came from. I let them remind me, not define me. There is a big difference between the two. It is a bit crazy to me that the scars I carry from losing nine toes bother me less than the ones I received as a defenseless child. I won! You can too!

~~~

Start each day

by saying something positive

to yourself.

It helps start you off in the right direction.

It will create a more

productive and successful

you.

~24~

FORWARD

If I could teach you
Just one thing
It would be to live
In your moment
Let your heart sing
The magic
We create in life
The happiness we bring
Endless possibilities
Experience everything
Do not waste your time
On those who do not see
That life is a gift
That special journey in life
A chosen destiny
So walk the path you chose
Let nothing hold you back
This life you have been blessed to live
Will help you learn to give back

When you are walking your path giving, receiving, and paying it forward, you are creating a balance. A flow of energy around you. It is a contagious energy that others are often attracted to. This can be great for you to help others on their chosen paths. This can also be a hindrance to you on your own chosen path. There has to be a balance when helping others. We are not allowed to help more than necessary. We can assist, guide, and encourage, but do not take another person off of their meant to be journey or ignore the path you walk by becoming too consumed in another person's situation. It is always a clearer picture to us when we view somebody else's dilemma, which is why we willingly leave our own task and want to help that other person. We can easily see what needs to be fixed or how to fix it. However, the way you would fix something in another person's life, may not be how they should fix it for the betterment of theirs. Keep your fixing to your own path and share the lessons you have learned from your experience. Help them learn to make a better choice, for that choice is theirs to make, not yours. Helping someone for your own personal gain is a no-no as well. It is not going to make you a better soul if you are doing it for all the wrong reasons. I wish there were a way for me to help every person on this planet. If I could find a universal way for us to find that one common denominator, that one connection could bring us all together in world peace, you know I would have shared it by now! As I smile at this, I also know He sent me back to help people. He never told me to come back and make the world be one, or at peace with each other. I happen to have a very goal oriented mind, so it never hurts to dream! Really though, as long as humankind has the freedom of choice for the growth of their own soul, I will continue to share my story and the lessons I have learned. If what I have lived through can shine a light on one of you, or give you the power to make a positive change in your life, then everything I have suffered through will have been worth the pain. My pain is my reminder of why I came back. Had I made the choice to stay on the other side, I would have no pain, but I also would surely have felt very unfulfilled. My soul has grown immensely since I returned to my body and embraced the path of my destiny.

It is important to know, understand, and recognize the hindrances to this kind of situation. It is easy for you to become a target to people who are looking to feel better, but do not want to do the work for themselves. A positive person can be used and manipulated into helping for all the wrong reasons. Be aware! Listen to your deep intuition. Living your purpose is very attractive to other people. Be truthful and helpful, but do not be tricked and taken advantage of. Learn to tell the difference. This can save you so much wasted time and heartache. I am not being negative by telling you this, it happened to me on several occasions until I learned to recognize what was happening. I am now completely aware of fake opportunists who have the wrong intention. It is a lesson I had to learn the hard way. Beware, but be kind. Teach yourself to listen to your intuition, you will learn to recognize when you need to be on guard.

~~~

Intuition

Listen to what yours is trying to tell you.

Gut feelings

The hairs standing up on the back of you neck.

Inner voice

The goosebumps that pop up on your arms.

A dream

The vision of something you need to be

aware of.

Whatever the feelings, acknowledge them.

Pay attention to what they are trying to tell you.

~25~

CHOOSE

Choose the lighted path
That leads you to your purpose
You will feel the knowing inside
Of destiny unfolding
A spark then a flame
It's your moment, so shine
No matter what
Pay attention to the signs
Your guidance will surround you
For that is what leads you
Knowing inside
They will never deceive you
An ounce of passion
Inside your mind
Can create the destiny
That you are trying to find
Let your faith lead you
No doubt of the time
For your future is before you
Waiting for you
To decide

Choose. The number one thing to help move you forward on your destined path is choosing to move forward. It is time for you to let go of your doubt, let the inner knowing of your passion give you the needed push, and propel into the meant to be purpose of your life. Do not make this harder than it has to be. You do have a choice, so no excuses. Make up your mind and make it happen. The vast amount of time wasted in your life is by procrastination. If you don't know, search inward. If you are afraid, find a way to kick the fear out of your mind. Have faith! Remind your conscious mind that you are taking over! You will not be held back by fear any longer. You have a life to live. Search inward to find your true abilities. Let the spark within you be ignited into a burning passion. Society is not the cause of you not being accomplished in life, you are. You have the ability to defy all the odds that have been stacked up against you. Like building blocks, you only need to remove the stack sitting in front of your path. You do not need to figure out how to move the building.

There is a simple conversation of just a few questions I like to have with people on a regular basis. What age are you? Do you think, based on the age you are right now, that your life has passed its halfway point? If I get a dazed look, it usually warrants a response from me. Have your never thought of this before? Most generally, I get "no", "yes", and "I don't know", "I never thought of it that way". I usually say, what are you waiting for? Your life is passing you by. Why do you think you were sent here? Let's figure it out. It is your choice, so, choose. Choose to live out the things you want to be known and remembered for. Choose the adventurous dream that burned inside you at a young age, before life's pressures replaced your passions. Choose to get on track with your time and be who you were meant to be. You have to be the one to choose. It is amazing that once a choice is made, the doors seem to open. The avenues of that path are opening as if they have just been waiting for you to decide.

If you have spent a number of years doubting yourself it may also take a mind adjustment before you move forward. This is simply because doubt has a stronger control on your thoughts and forward progression, more so than a positive thought. We are kings and queens of talking ourselves out of success. Kick that doubt to the curb, adjust your thoughts, and go get it!

~~~

Empowering the new you.

Do not be afraid

to ask questions,

seek answers,

or search for the truth.

The knowledge you attain

will enlighten and improve

the new you.

~26~

RAIN

I feel the seasons
Changing now
The one that most alarms me
My fear runs deep
As my heart skips a beat
As thunder clouds build above me
My anxiety heightens
As my mind tries to focus
On the situation that lies before me
Year after year
Spring after spring
My dreams to this day still haunt me
I'll survive again
I know this is fact
As I prepare my nerves
For that first loud crack
The vibration will shake me
Way deep inside
I will fight my instinct
To run and hide
I won't let fear control me
Nor question my mind
What peace I have found
Wasn't easy to find

Storm season, my toughest time of year. I will not lie, it still affects me but I know that I will not allow it to define me. It will only remind me of my meant to be journey. I may not be hiding under the bed or on the floorboard of the car anymore, but the fact is, I still have that fear creep into my mind. I feel the anxiety sweat wash over me and I have a tough time controlling my breathing. At that point I have to make my mind go into a controlled conversation with myself, one that I have had many times over. "God, you promised to protect and watch over me, so don't even think about making me get through this alone. I need to feel the protection of the guidance that you have placed around me." As I talk this through my mind I am able to calm down, relax, and wait for the storms to pass. See, even I still have lessons to learn! We should never stop striving to be better.

Every spring, this is how I felt. Fear! At times it has overwhelmed me. All I wanted to do was hide, cry, and run from it. Anything to make the recurring fear inside me stop. I would have nightmares that have felt as though I was reliving the experience and think that there was no way for me to survive. It overwhelmed me and consumed my thoughts. I feared I would be struck again. It took me a very long time to gather the tools I needed to take back my control over my emotional turmoil. After doctors, medications, meditation, counseling, bio-feedback, hypnotism, massage, prayers, begging my Creator to make the fear stop, and anything else I could think of to try, I decided I was not going to be the victim of this fear for the rest of my life. I had no choice except to choose to learn how to survive my own life experience. I owned it, the experience didn't own me! After gathering what worked for me, from all the avenues mentioned above, I took what made sense to me and applied it to my life of healing. I became my own hunter and gatherer. My route became victim to survivor. I challenged myself with small goals. I allowed myself to take baby steps. It may have taken me longer to accomplish things, but the baby steps allowed me to not give up. I told myself daily that everything was possible. Today I am able to celebrate the progress I have made. Although the nightmares have their own schedule and show up when they want to, I do not back down from the fight. I do not allow them to consume me or my thoughts. I have learned that the fear of something can also give me strength.

The storm I speak of here can be applied to any situation which has given you a feeling of fear or anxiety.

~~~

Start a new path to personal

self-improvement.

Realize that you are venturing onto a path of

self-focus.

You must get into the habit of paying attention

to you.

It is not being selfish, but self-improving, that will change

the way you see yourself.

Then, it is the self-empowered person

you have become that others will see in you.

~27~

NIGHTMARE

When darkness surrounds you
Take a deep breath down
Let it give you some balance
Let your brain calm down
When darkness surrounds you
'Till you just want to explode
Take a step back
Don't let your mind go rogue
When darkness surrounds you
Black magic tempting your mind
Just take a deep breath
Don't let this dharma unwind
When I'm running blind
I need some help to see
What's inside of me
That black magic tempting me
Is this my destiny
Step back
A gasp for breath
No worries
Just another bad dream

PTSD stands for Post Traumatic Stress Disorder. This is what I was diagnosed with. I had no control over my nightmares. The amount of searching I did to make them stop was like searching for the voodoo queen herself. It seemed as though I was willing to try anything to bring my brain back to a normal realm of function. There is no way for me to explain this diagnosis. I have never found the words to describe it fully, if you have been there of course, then you know. I am just unable to describe it clearly. I know that I was not able to control the fear I had inside my mind while I was reliving the experience. I had doctors who placed me on anti-depressants, anti-anxiety, and pain medications. Nothing made it stop. Those medications can help people when a medical condition is also in play, but for me, they were unsuccessful.

Obviously, I just had a massive amount of nightmares. Who wouldn't after being hit with lightning twice? Your brain has a way of traveling through the things you fear the most. It was as though the fear was feeding the experience to attract it to me again. I could be running through my nightmares for miles with lightning bolts crashing left, right, behind, and out in front of me. They would pick me up and toss me across the ground. I was unable to pull myself awake. There was nothing I could do to remove myself from it, so I would keep running and screaming, begging for anyone to hear me and help me. There was never anyone else there to help me back. I have never felt as completely alone in all of my life as I did through those first years of my recovery. So, I kept running and surviving on my own until I made it through the maze of it all. I would jolt awake, disoriented by my surroundings. I felt as though some ancient curse had taken part in my today life. It was all so confusing to my living days of healing. I just wanted it to stop! I was so tired from running through my nightmares that I hardly had the energy to make it through my days. Again, I made a conscious decision to take all that I had gathered, learned, and put it into action. I set a goal to conquer my fears. I was not going to accept being driven by fear for the rest of my life.

The subject of PTSD is not a very comfortable one for a person who is trying to survive it. It is confusing. It hurts, and no matter how many people tell you to get over it, you can't seem to figure out how. It would be like me telling you to forget something awful you saw yesterday, and all it makes you do is remember it more. Imagine that times one thousand. For me, and I will only speak for myself, it was like a flashback of a nightmare, day or night, awake or sleeping, and it had no boundaries. It would invade my mind. It could be triggered by a storm, a firecracker sound, or a knock too loud on the door. I have yet to figure out what triggered it in my sleep.

If you know someone dealing with this leftover trauma, be patient with them. PTSD can be an all-consuming condition. One that makes you question every detail and every reality, just to make sure that you are still alive, not just living in a nightmare. If your person is willing, you can help them log the triggers. Write about the effects it is having on them and start finding the connections to the original incident. After gathering the pieces that became broken and fragmented, your person can find an acceptable balance of healing. It may never return to the exact way it was before, but without trying, you will never know what you could have reclaimed of yourself. Remind yourself that a normal person's life changes and they can't turn the clock back to be who they were yesterday either. All I do know is that the healing balance is possible. I am still surviving it.

~~~

Only I can share with you my experience with PTSD. I am trying to share a few tools that I have gathered. They have helped improve my journey with it. I know that it is a complicated experience. In my heart I have deep compassion for every soldier, every victim, and every person who has had a traumatic experience so bad that it has turned into this. I know I do not have all the answers, but I wanted you to know that I do relate to and understand another person's emotional entrapment as they are going through this. My desire is that you find some peace as you learn the skills to heal these inner wounds and survive. Please, do not allow this to hold you down as the victim of uncontrollable circumstance.

~28~

PAIN

As I walk my path in life
With pain you may not see
A journey of learning to cope
Like I'm a butterfly
With broken wings
Whether my pain is deep inside
Or a scrape across the knee
A person's pain should not be judged
By another human being
For me it is encompassing
Surrounding my entire being
Forcing me to take control
Of things you cannot see
My pain is as fragile
As that butterfly who's flying free
Each day I have to take a chance
Persuade myself to believe
I exist in mind over matter
Holding on, to my hopes and dreams
Sometimes this pain tries to bury me
Some days it makes me scream
I have taught myself to hide it well
So others do not see
As I watch the flight of the butterfly
I can imagine it carrying me
To another place
Where I can exist
And this pain
Can be set free

I know that pain is a factor in many people's lives. Definitely not an easy one to overcome. I can relate to pain in so many ways, on so many levels, as if I have my own messed up relationship with it. Seriously, my pain from the lightning has been with me longer than I have been married to my husband. I wish I could pack its bags and move it out to the curb! Break up with it for good! I have tried and it doesn't work. The only thing left is to make it work between you and it. Find a way to exist and be productive through it. I'll admit it is not an easy journey, but if its going to be with you, like an ugly set of luggage, find a way to make it presentable. I am not a person who likes to complain, but pain can make you ugly, too. I also am not someone who can be medicated throughout each day. Some can and that is fine if it works for them, however, it just doesn't work well with my goals. I have too many things to accomplish in what time I have left on this Earth plane. There are meditations and relaxation techniques I have found that help most. I also wake up each morning and have a chat with my pain, so to speak. I get it in control. I acknowledge its existence in my life, thank it for the lessons, and make it go to the back of the closet. Since I started taking this approach to the ugly luggage, I have been able to be more productive. I still have everyday pain and even on my severe pain days, I just allow less of it to disrupt my life.

If you are in the same situation as me, allow me to suggest a few possible ways for you to gain the upper hand on your pain. First, you must decide to be in control of it and not allow it to control you. Find a level in your pain that is functional to your everyday life. If you are medicating the pain away, you are only masking it. Finding a way to compartmentalize the pain will allow you to function in the midst of it without letting it control your life.

Pain can be physical, emotional, or mental. No matter the reason for it, pain still has to be looked at and dealt with in order for you to productively exist in your life.

If it is emotional or mental pain, I want you to realize that the things that you have experienced have made you who you are today. You only need to view each lesson, maybe try writing them down, to help see the pattern that has been created in your life from the first emotional experience. There is always a pattern, from the first to the present. You may be re-experiencing and allowing the repeat cycle. It is up to you to recognize this, take the lesson that you are meant to learn, and stop the dysfunctional flow. Once you find the lesson then let go of the emotional pain that is associated with what you have experienced. It is not meant for you to carry the pain through your entire lifetime in your ugly luggage bag. It's only for you to learn what you are meant to learn from it. That will also help you in the future to recognize and acknowledge that you won't allow yourself to go through it again.

For physical pain, I have also found that writing it down and figuring out the connection of each pain is crucial. For example, I have had 9 toes amputated. This has a connective effect on the pain from my legs and into my feet. When I am focused on my amputated portions, I am missing the connection. I have learned to see the body as a whole. I will focus the healing energy at the upper portion of my legs and work my way down. I use certain oils and lotions which have a calming effect on the nerve damage and blood flow. Massaging and stretching the muscles keeps the blood flowing to the extremities so that I am keeping them as healthy as I can. It is a choice, either exist in the pain or search to find acceptable ways to really live through the pain. You have the upper hand in your relationship with it, don't allow it to have that control over you.

~~~

If I did not know pain,

how would I ever appreciate

the days that I am blessed enough

to have none?

~29~

LIES

Do not be a liar
Do not be a cheat
What goes around
Will come around
I'm warning you to think
Your blatant contradictions
The white lies that you speak
What I see
What you think
Are two very different things
I'm trying to wake you up
Just trying to help you see
That if you do not change your ways
Your ship is going to sink
Your lies are catching up to you
The twisted ways you scheme
What will be the catalyst
That loses you everything

Liars and cheaters are people I do not want to be around. I would rather not breath the same air as them. I just can't seem to wrap my understanding around a person who chooses to lie, cheat, or be deceitful for their own personal gain. As human beings, we are predisposed to trust people. We make decisions through our emotions instead of our logic. Too often, we trust the wrong people.

Whether in a relationship, a business deal, or for whatever situation, the lies will eventually catch up to you. It truly has a devastating affect on the person who has been deceived.

Nearly every day, I read something or hear of someone being scammed, lied to, and taken advantage of. As we get older we want to help and believe in others more profoundly. That is wonderful! However, we are so willing to be helpful that we are becoming blind to when we are being used. When your gut feelings are trying to warn you of the contradicting information you are getting, pay attention! Wake up. A person who lies and cheats, has no conscience.

I believe in karma, just as I believe in fate. If you lie, cheat, or steal, you will meet the fate of living through the karma you deserve. That will come in the form of a life lesson, probably not a very pleasant one. It will be a karmic life lesson that your choices have opened the door to.

I do not want to ever experience one of those, so the decision is mine to make the right choice in the first place. We are taught right from wrong in our youth and we have an inner knowing. The excuse of "I didn't know" just doesn't work for me coming from an adult. Every one of us knows the difference between right and wrong and good versus bad. We have to make a choice as to which one is the path that we want to live. When you know and you choose, you accept the consequences to your choices and your actions.

There really are genuine people out there who do want to help, but don't be naive. Keep your vigilance. Protect yourself from the predatory sweet talkers who cross your path. Truth is one of my passions. I will definitely hurt someone with the truth, rather than tell them a lie.

Lies hurt and hold a person back from their forward progression. Being cheated on by the person you proclaim to love can strip another human being of their self-esteem, their dignity, and any self-worth they had inside. It can take years for a person to rebuild the parts of themselves that a cheater has destroyed by his or her choices. I will say this, if you are cheating, you are doing something very damaging to the other person. End things and allow them their dignity, do not strip them of every bit of pride or self-esteem they have. If you feel you are going to cheat, leave your other person first!

If you can, choose to do your own self a favor; then tell the truth, always.

~~~

Wave your red umbrella

in the air so I can see

the next person on my path

of my next meant to be.

The red umbrella is like a light.

It shines through the nights pure darkness.

From a mountain top

a place in space

or an evening of mist.

It is my beacon, it is my sign.

It is how I am guided to find

you.

~30~

DRIFTING

As apart we drift
Like frothy bubbles
To the waters edge
We float away in silence
Not knowing
If the emotional tides
That carry us
Into the unknown
Will ever bring us back
Together again
We vowed to be one
With each other
True lovers and friends
Never doubting
The love that we have
For one another
Never envisioning an end
The depths of this water
As it carries us forth
Is like drowning in our own
Emotional growth
Alone
As communication
Has been lost

Relationships can be ever changing, like the tides that roll across the seas. They can also slip slowly into an abyss of darkness that you had no inkling of until it crashes over the waterfall. They can also be like little bubbles on a lake, just softly floating apart as two people forget to include each other in their daily moments. We can often become so busy in our routines that we don't take the time to give a gentle touch or an encouraging word to our spouses. It happens way too often. I can tell you, it takes more time for couples to reconnect than it took them to disconnect. Rebuilding something is a whole lot harder than reminding yourself to stay connected to your relationship as you go. I have couples say to me, "I don't know how we drifted apart or what went wrong." All I can say is that you forgot to pay attention. Wake up! Pay attention! Do not allow your relationship to get to that point. Pay attention to each other. Communicate with your person. Truly listen to what your person has to say. Marriage doesn't have to be hard! Be respectful, kind, and encouraging to the person you vowed to love. The drift apart starts when we are too busy to even talk. Communication connects the two of you and helps relieve doubt and stress. If you stay consciously aware of keeping your foundation solid in your relationship the stresses of daily life will not be able to crack the foundation beneath you.

It is just fine for two people to have separate interests in their relationship, but you must also have some connective ones. I think it is very healthy to have some individual friends you can enjoy doing things with that your partner may not be interested in. It is the nourishment for each persons interests that keeps the relationship in balance. It should never become one sided. For instance, I love to look for rocks and spend a significant amount of my time helping other people on their journeys. My husband loves football and hardly ever has much to say in regards to advice for others, but he will secretly buy a meal for a family while he is out to lunch. We have our separate interests, but together, we both have a passion for helping others. We both love music and long rides on a motorcycle. We have found that connective balance to keep our relationship strong while still supporting individual passions.

If it is jealousy of your partner that keeps you from having separate time, reevaluate your relationship. Trust must be present in order for the relationship to be healthy from the beginning. This can be a very difficult thing to overcome if you have brought past hurt into a new relationship. This is part of what I have previously mentioned. The pain must be healed and let go of to move forward, or you will repeat the same scenario.

I was taught a long time ago the only person which you have the full ability to change in this lifetime is you. If you are trying to control your partner and change them, trying to make them be what and who you want them to be, it will go nowhere. It is bound for an unhappy ride. You may as well end it now, because you are never going to make another human being be exactly who or what you want them to be. Go and find the person you are trying to change them into!

When you find the person who has a connection to you you will feel it. It is a different feeling, or a knowing, that this is right. It just works without you having to make the pieces fit together. I am constantly reminding people that we are all here for a reason. It is a wonderful feeling to find another soul who shares your interests, but allow them to have their own as well, for they also have individual lessons to learn, not just the ones that you may want them to see in your way.

~~~

Allow yourself the pleasure,

of a deliciously sweet dessert.

Everything in life

is controlled with moderation.

So a taste now and then,

will not hurt.

~31~

OBSTACLES

Life is not always
About what we want
We need to recognize
The powers above
As things won't move forward
To give us the answers we seek
Step out of the emotion
Take an honest peek
At what lies before us
Are the obstacles trying to speak
The journey that we travel
Those lessons that we force
May not be what is best
For our souls real growth
Continue on with caution
Do not be deceived
Sometimes what we want in life
Should never, ever be

Are the obstacles in your path trying to tell you something? Are they keeping you from running into a bad situation or trying to help you avoid something that could be life changing in a negative way? Are you trying to force an action before it is time for it to happen? Slow down. Stop. Step out of the emotion of the situation. Allow yourself to look at things from a different place. Ask yourself why and really allow the answer to reveal itself to you. We search for the answers and still try to keep control of the situation at the same time. You should not force the change to occur while you are ignoring the obstacles in front of you. Your guidance is trying to tell you something. They may be trying to help you avoid an undesirable life changing result, but if you keep choosing not to see, it will be you who gets to deal with the consequences of these changes. No matter how badly we may want something or how hard we try to force something to happen in our lives. We must remind ourselves that everything happens when it is supposed to happen, in the time that it is meant to happen. Allow yourself to see the obstacles being placed in your path, may help you avoid a hard road ahead.

We have freedom of choice in this life. You can always move ahead onto a path that will take you places. One that will challenge you, where you can still come out a winner. However, if that path wasn't something you had to experience, why waste the time on your journey? You could have been experiencing something much more enlightening and meaningful to your soul's growth.

I believe that divine intervention comes in many forms. It can be a divine warning sign, a divine obstacle, or even a divine person who has been placed into your life to help you in much bigger ways. I have experienced all three. I have been placed into other people's lives to help them along the way. It is a sense of knowing, a recognition, that this has to be something bigger than me. If you allow yourself to look back over your life and your struggles, you may recognize there were signs. People who passed through your life may have tried to help you when you needed it most. Maybe it was a phone call that delayed your day that might have helped you avoid something. Maybe a friend contacted you from your past. Maybe they just wanted you to know that they were thinking about you. Maybe it was the one phone call that saved your life that day. The signs can show themselves in so many different forms. It is up to each individual to be open minded to the signs that are appearing all around them. You could find a simple penny on the ground. It could be a penny from heaven, a sign from a loved one, or a feeling that passes over you for luck. It could be a feather on your path, a connective feeling that your loved one who has passed is showing you a sign for hope. It could be a butterfly landing on your lap to show you change, a new beginning, or a door opening to a new you. It may be a loved one passing over you in flight, just to give you the feeling that you are not alone. Whatever the sign may be, acknowledge it. Open yourself to the possibility that your signs and obstacles are being placed around you for a reason. You will become aware that they have been showing themselves to you so much more often than you realized. You will feel a new sense of self and a knowing that you are not alone.

~~~

I sometimes may be colorblind

To your twisted wicked lies

As the thunder beats

And the raven sings

You'd be wise to know

That there will always be

An inner strength in me

Since I already know

I am not walking alone

~32~

UGHHHHHHH

Ten deep breaths
You can't control the actions of others
No matter how hard you try
Even when the action taken
Leaves you wanting to cry
The kindness in me
Is what I wish to see
In others who
Choose to deceive
When what is left
Is a hole in my chest
Where my believing heart
Used to be
As my faith reminds me
That my truth matters more
Than the twisted ways
Of those others
I will find my peace
In the remedies
That I create from my lessons
Once more

Yes, make yourself breath. When the outcome of a situation depends on more than just you following through, just breath. More often than I care to admit, I have allowed myself to become disappointed in a situation where my expectation was different than the outcome. Remember, everything happens for a reason, in the time it is meant to happen. It does not matter how badly we want something to work out. If it is a meant to be in our lives, it will happen when it is supposed to happen. When we get to caught up in our destination, we tend to disregard the warning signs. If you are being warned at every turn, step back and really analyze those signs. It is usually for a very good reason that things aren't working out. It is part of the lesson to first recognize the signs. Second is to be willing to let go of the want and let things land where they are meant to. I know that this sounds easy, however, we have all been there. When the want overrules common sense, we have a problem. Even I have worked through every warning sign, smoothed out all of my obstacles, and still ended up with a massive road block, seemingly out of nowhere. That was the moment I realized I was not paying attention.

If I truly believed in meant to be, I had to stop the progression in the direction I was heading in. At some point the signs would have stopped and I would have forced an outcome to the very thing that I was ignoring. I would have had an experience that may have been disastrous to me and my family.

In the process of forcing what you may want, it is important to really be aware of the energy of those around you. There are those who may be trying to sabotage your destination out of jealousy. I'm not saying to become paranoid about people, I'm simply stating that not every one around you will always have your back or the best intentions toward your goal. If what you are trying to achieve becomes something another person desires it could derail your own journey's destination. Choose your friends wisely.

In the end, I have come to realize that being truthful and faithful to those around me is what matters most. I will take the lessons I am meant to experience from those people who still choose to deceive, but I will come out on the other side of the experience with more knowledge and armor for my next meant to be lesson. I will not let it harm me, for we all had a part in the journey we had to walk together, regardless of the outcome.

~~~

Sometimes not getting what you want

can be the biggest blessing in life.

It doesn't matter why.

Only know that it may have saved you

from something you were unable to see.

You are standing exactly where

you are supposed to be.

~33~

KEYS

I have this ring of keys
A hundred doors
All locked
But each one visible to me
A choice to be made
An effort to see
The door that leads
To my meant to be
No choice will be wrong
Each door holds a clue
A sign posted
Showing me
What I am meant to do
A map of sorts
That leads me to
Help other souls
Will my next door be you

We are all given keys in life or clues to the doors we should walk through. They are signs on our journey, a dream, or a desire that pushes us to go for something we want to achieve. As you assess your life and look at the keys you hold in your hand, you are acknowledging that you hold the power of choice towards your own direction. Whatever key you choose to use will ultimately take you through a very different door, to a very different experience. The most rewarding part of this whole life journey is the fact that you get to choose your next door.

After my lightning experience; I had many keys to doors that I felt were not taking me to where I wanted to be. I now realize that I gathered something from each one of them. Whether the most mundane experience or the most profound, you will learn and gather something useful to you that will help you on another part of your journey.

As I've said before, I knew that I would write these books since I was 18 years old. I have taken the long road to get here. I had to gather the pieces by walking through doors which may have seemed as though they were in the wrong building, but I needed something to reconnect me with the destiny path that is now in front of me. I woke up early one day and I knew it was time to start my destiny path. I knew that I had finally gathered what I needed most. As I walked around in my dream, I knew I had walked out of a door and as I looked back, I saw that the word written on it was "suffering." I saw the keys in my hand, I looked around to see so many doors to choose from. There it was, my new door. The door that would lead me to my prosperity, my life goals, my life of commitment to do what I had been asked to come back here to do. My key opened the door to my future. Now, don't be misguided by the word prosperity. I know that it comes in many forms such as faith, friends, family, and kindness. To be prosperous is to be rich in many forms of life. I was ready to share the knowledge and faith, as well as pain and tragedies I had suffered through. I want to show how they can walk into their light of knowing their destiny, and ultimately, their prosperity.

As God knows, I had suffered for long enough. Since there is no room for regrets in my life, I can say that there is nothing I would ever change. I would not change a single one of my experiences, for without them my life would be lacking a tool, or perhaps a key, to allow me to help somebody else on their journey. I still have great pain in my body; that is not all that my suffering was about. My suffering was a combination of everything. All of my experiences, the cataloguing of them, the understanding of them, the relationship, and bonds that I had to form with them were necessary. Without any one of them, I would still be searching for a missing piece of my puzzle. I have learned the coping skills that I was in need of to exist prosperously with my pain. Remember, you can teach yourself to compartmentalize the pain. It does not get to be the ruler of your world, unless you allow it to. Of course, you have that choice. Like everything you choose to experience, what you allow to affect you the most will be what teaches you the greatest lesson.

~~~

Today I want you to lose yourself, in you.

Get lost in the right direction.

For the first time in your life,

simply allow yourself

to do it, for you and no one else.

For there is absolutely no one else

who will appreciate your happiness

more than you.

~34~

I AM

Somebody's
Granddaughter
Daughter
Mother
Sister
Niece
Aunt
Cousin
Spouse
Friend
Teacher
Mentor
Counselor
I am
Someone
Therefore
I am
Somebody

Everybody is somebody. I am forever saddened by the ones who believe that they are nobody. They convince themselves that their life has no connection, meaning, or that they have no direction.

I am here to say that you are somebody. Your life does matter. No matter how you came to believe this doubtful thing about yourself, it is not true. Today is the day you change that thought about you. Make a list on your tablet. Go ahead and make your negative list first to get it out of the way:

~ Negative Examples
- No confidence
- Self-doubting

Now, draw your line down the middle of your page for the positives. This list is to show where we are heading. People tend to forget that they even have a positive side while residing in their negative. Really search and be honest with yourself.

~ Positive Examples
- Creative
- Compassionate
- Kind
- Good at listening
- Loving
- Trustworthy
- Faithful
- Good friend

Give yourself some credit here and really find the beautiful qualities about you. Realize the true things make you somebody. Do not allow the negative things that others have convinced you of to penetrate this list. This is your side of the paper, not theirs. This is where you will spend the most amount of your time truly searching for your new way of living. You are giving yourself permission to redefine the way you see yourself. You are somebody!

When you spend all your time doubting yourself, you are really doubting God. Your Creator made you in the image of Himself. Do you not think that it is detrimental to your well-being for you to start seeing yourself in a more positive light? To start taking responsibility for your own direction? To start living the life you were meant to accomplish? I do! The first place to begin is in your own mind. Stop believing every negative thing about you. Stop hiding behind your own insecurity of becoming more than you are today. You can do this. Living and experiencing life is why you are here, not to just passively exist in your own doubt. Forget about the things that held you back yesterday. Start a new way of living today. Tomorrow is going to be exactly what you make it. So why not make it extraordinary? Really start cherishing the time you have left to make your life as memorable as you want it to be. Stop existing in the victim role. Be the somebody I already know you are.

~~~

I wish you peace to balance your energy.

I wish you vision to find what you seek.

I wish you light to shine on your journey.

I wish you courage, to not be afraid.

I wish you faith to trust where you're going.

I wish you knowledge to see when you arrive.

~35~

REGRETS

Living with regrets
Can make you feel so broken
As days pass you by
Your desires go unspoken
Make an honest effort
Just to help you see
The soul living through you
Needs to be set free
Your journey is for experiencing
The path, of your meant to be
When you retreat
Into your hiding place
Out of fear or anxiety
It only proves
Your lack of faith
That He will stand by thee
As I will set out
To help you see
The path
Of your meant to be

Today we are going to set forth on a new path. Get out your pen and paper. Highlight the things that stand out to you. After all, this book of lessons is for you. This will be your new door, it can be opened to a new you. You will no longer allow yourself to be held back by your own regrets, or the things you wish you would have done. This is your wake up call. It is your life, your journey, and your path of choices. It is time to stop living in fear of starting to move forward. That fear is what is creating your regrets. When we remove the fear of rejection, not being good enough, or that no one will ever love us, only then can we begin a new cycle of awareness. You will empower your spirit by becoming more confident in yourself. This is not a difficult journey, it may have just seemed as if it was impossible to change because of your fear, but you have the tools. You have opened your eyes, your mind, and your new door. Now you are ready. There is nothing to be afraid of.

You are now going to write down everything that you know you need to let go of, all the things that have held you back.

~ Examples:
- Self-doubt
- Following other peoples expectations of you
- Not able to love
- Negative people around you

These negative aspects in your life are drawing a map on paper for you to follow. Continue to add explanations of each negative point you have written down. As you become more aware of your changes, you will start to see the negatives turn into positives. Those positives will be reflected in your life.

On another piece of paper write down your dreams and desires, even the ones you have never spoken of out loud to anyone. Those deepest desires are the ones that lead to your passion. With those written down, make a list of the tools that you want to gather to make your dreams, desires, and passions become more powerful. Positives will cancel out more of your negatives.

You can also make a list of your most powerful qualities. These are the aspects of yourself that you will build your new foundation on. Give yourself credit here also. You are not allowed to beat yourself up anymore or feel guilty for looking at what is best about you. Life changes start with you. Figuring out your journey of meant to be is a selfish and selfless act rolled up into one. Truly finding who you were meant to be is the best gift in life that you can give to yourself and those who encompass the space around you.

~ Examples:
- Communication skills
- Ability to focus on details
- Great personality
- Loving nature

By acknowledging your strengths, you are adding direction to your map and building a much stronger foundation for you to stand on. As you gather your tools needed, the positive confidence builds and you will start your movement forward.

Please don't make this harder than it is. We put up our own roadblocks and allow them to be the answer that stops our forward progression. It is alright to hear the word no! It should make you stronger and more determined. Do not allow a no to close the road ahead of you. It just means that this place or thing was not your meant to be. Acknowledge that!

Passion in your life takes perseverance. It is solely up to you to not to give up. You must find the strength and determination from deep inside, along with knowing that nothing can stop you. You are better than what has ever been acknowledged by others, including you. Block the negative and put a light of energy around you. Hold your battle shield like a warrior. Raise your arm and yell, "I am worth it!" You are worth the effort that it will take to find you again. You did not become broken in a single second of time. It took time to let it all slip away from you. Now is your time to take it back. You are going to tape, glue, and nail yourself back together until you are fully mended. Never doubt that you are worth everything your life can offer. Change means growth! Do not fear your changes!

~~~

Celebrate, love, and embrace yourself.

~36~

PURPOSE

I had
An amazing dream
Where you showed me
The purpose of my being
The meaning of my life
Of who I'm meant to be
I know it's worth the time
It's taken for me to see
Everything
That is meant for me
To learn, to teach, to be
We are not forgotten
Just often, forget to see
A structure of our universe
The dot that connects
You to me
Take a moment, to realize
The powers above, will be
The one thing
That connects us all
To the knowing
Of our true meant to be
Embrace your purpose
Be guided by your passion
Only then, will you see
That you are living
Not just existing
In your own
Amazing Dream

Dream of your purpose, really see what your true meant to be is. In order for you to manifest it, you must first learn to dream it. You cannot manifest something that you choose to not see. Visualize yourself doing exactly what you are dreaming of. When we surround ourselves with the positive thoughts of our dream we begin to see a living picture of it. A knowing emerges and the vibration of its energy encompasses our being. We begin to feel our purpose take form around us. You can create the outcome of your thoughts, negative or positive. So be vigilant, know that what thoughts you think can emerge in your life. For the good and bad, if all you do is doubt the outcome that you desire, then you will surround it in negativity. If you allow yourself to see it in your dream form and feed it positive thoughts, then you can see your positive direction.

We are not forgotten souls. We sometimes think that God is not hearing our prayers. It is us who often forget to see that the universe is trying to allow us to connect the dots to our own journeys. When you pray and then worry, you are not truly living in your faith. You are trying to control every aspect of your journey, without taking the time to let the answers to your prayers come through. Stop doing that! If you are searching for the answer, you must let it go in order for your answer to come through. Have faith! It may come as a sign, a dream, or even someone telling you out of the blue! Leave some room in your mind and heart for the answer to show itself to you. On whatever path you choose, there is no wrong direction if it is forward. However, when you are really seeking confirmation as to which path to travel, stop shopping for the only answer that you want to hear. Lend come credence to your own intuition. It is most likely trying to tell you something that you are ignoring. We seem to get so caught up in our dilemmas that we completely sabotage our own outcomes.

Remember, take the time to ask the question, then let it go. Try writing it down and placing it in your prayer jar. If you don't have one, make one. Decorate it up as fancy and awesome as you want. Put your positive energy into it as you are creating its beauty. It can even stay an ordinary pickle jar. It only matters to you and your prayers and questions. Put a date on the bottom of your jar. This is the day that you are making a change, your day to start trusting in you and your destiny. Let the answers come. Now close the lid tight so you won't be tempted to take it out and therefore take it back. You can add prayers to the jar, but do not read the ones that are already in there. I want you to go on about your day, your week, your month, and even your year. On your one year prayer jar anniversary, make a date with yourself to spend some time reading your prayers. Write down the answers that came to you as you were busy walking and living in your new trusting faith. I tried this many years ago and now I am the most believing, faithful person whom many people have ever met. The fact is, it works if you allow it to. It really is amazing how much stress this awesome little prayer jar takes off our shoulders.

This can also be something fun to do with your friends, church groups, book clubs, and even your children. This may help them learn at an earlier age to trust and know that they are not alone. It is a very functional tool to help you to let go.

~~~

A catalyst can create a whirlwind of change in everything around it.

Sometimes you are the catalyst creating the change around you.

Observe.

Acknowledge.

Is the universe trying to create a change around or within you?

~37~

AWAKENED

Sand castles wash away
And storm clouds, always break
The drama can be
Removed from your path
As very few things in this life
Are rarely left up to chance
You are here because of fate
Given a choice to make something great
An opportunity to realign your time
Gifted with a quiet place to rewind
I shared your path to remind you
To embrace all that life has to offer
As many souls were put into place
To guide you through your greatest pains
We've stitched your wounds
To let the healing start within you
I didn't give up, I followed through
Just as your Father asked me to do
I only hope that I awakened
Enough inside your mind
To help you see their true intention
From the other side
They want you to believe in yourself
That you can save the lives
Of those who have deep pain inside
A pain that you recognize
So now that you know
That there is something bigger
Than the view that you see

From the edge of the ledge
That you are used to standing on
Remember, they are keeping watch
For they are only a thought away
As our chapter in this book
Is coming to an end
I want you to know that your time within
My life was a blessing
I hope that I have helped you find
Your true purpose
It was there all the time

~~~

We all have angels, guides, and people around us to help us through the most difficult times in our lives. It only takes awareness to recognize that these were placed around you for a reason. Becoming aware and taking the time to acknowledge them will give you the energy needed to help you move through your lesson more easily. I'm not saying that the lesson will still not be hard, it is just that alone it could have been even harder.

I am a dreamer in every sense of the word. I always have been through my entire life so far. I dream. It may be the very thing that has helped me believe as deeply and faithfully as I do. I believe we have the power of choice and therefore can create the positive changes within each of us.

As far as dreams go, I know that mine are very real. I have had too many confirming accounts for me to ever doubt them. In general, I don't push my dreams onto others, however, sometimes life places the stars on a course of their own to line up exactly how they are meant to, enabling the dots to connect. It is then a persons choice to believe or not. Fate is not up to me, but I will be present in the knowledge that you are always placed where you are meant to be standing if the connection needs to be made. You never know who might be trying to make their presence known to a loved one from heaven.

I am also a person who wants to help others to believe in their dreams. I want to truly give their mind a boost of encouragement, sweep out their doubts, and help them see how amazing they really are. Low self-esteem seems to be a crossroad path for so many. One day, you either decide to change your game or you will exist in your misery for however long you choose. If what you are living in is better and stronger than your fear of moving on, then you will sit out this round. Eventually, you will wish you would have changed your tactics. It is never too late.

Imagine if I were to tell you that your life was so important to saving the lives of others or that the message you will bring to them will ultimately make a critical difference in how others will live and view their lives. Would you consider making a change? Would the betterment of others inspire you to fulfill your meant to be? Would you let go of the fear that is holding you back, just so you could be that inspiration to somebody else? It could be that the very person you help is feeling precisely the same way as you were just feeling. Your life experience is always experienced for a reason. The connection will cross your path.

~~~

I will no longer be vulnerable

to my own negative thoughts

of how others perceive me.

~38~

STRESS

Overwhelmed
By the burdens sitting upon you
Consumed
By the worries of what lies before you
Haunted
By emotions of all who count on you
Restricted
By the ability to do anything about it
You've walked this road
Change
How you allow others to affect you
Choose
To let go of the worries you see before you
Believe
In the souls who have been placed around you
Release
The restrictions, that you have given power to
You no longer have to walk that road
It is you
You are the one, holding you back
All you have to do
Is let go

As you step onto the new path of discovering you, I want you to remember a few things. Stress comes in many forms. When you take on all the stresses you can find you are taking yourself off of your own path. It is up to you to find your technique, whatever works best for you, to relax. You are no longer going to take on the worries of the world. It is your responsibility to take care of yourself first. If you are not balanced in your right place you are not going to be able to help others. Make yourself a priority. Giving yourself permission to find that balance is not a selfish act. It is a healthy choice you are making to be better. You will become a more   pleasant person to be around. A person can hardly recognize the stress they release onto those around them. When you let go of this the people around you will become more relaxed as well.

~ Remind yourself:

- Each one of us is different
- We all have our own dreams
- There is a passion in each one of us
- It is up to each of us to find the purpose that is meant for us

- You, and only you, have the power to change
- You are allowed expectation in just yourself
- Everything you do is worth doing your best
- Leave nothing to chance
- Make life changes one baby step at a time
- Your life is what you make it
- Stop making excuses
- Decide what and who you want to become
- The weight of the world does not rest on your shoulders
- Time is your only enemy
- There is no room for fear in your life
- Be grateful and become great
- Who you are today does not define who you can become tomorrow
- Redefining yourself is on you
- You are no longer a victim
- You are now a survivor
- Change starts within you
- Your success can only be defined by yourself
- Happiness does not come from others around you, it creates itself from acceptance of you
- Learn to trust yourself, for if you never figure out how to do that, you will never truly trust anyone else
- Wake up your brain! It is time to find the connection between your brain's common sense and your soul's true essence

~~~

Go write down your feelings

of this grief inside of you.

This emotion that you feel inside

will create a new side of you.

An understanding

of time on your journey.

The inspiration to live your life

before your last breath

escapes from your chest,

and your time passes you by.

~39~

TRUST

I have this little bucket
It's filled with trust inside
I only take some out
When another crosses a line
I give my trust willingly
So it is up to the other to decide
To be the one
That has faith in us
Not be sneaky, or try to hide
For when my bucket is empty
You no longer will be tied
To the one that trusted
Whose heart is now broken
As I will refill
What is empty inside
I will do my best
Not to carry this over
To the next person
Who walks by my side
It is not their fault
That another person emptied
The trust bucket
That I carry inside

Oh, the pesky little bucket of trust! Why does this seem to be the number one emotional downfall of so many relationships? Ding, ding, ding! The answer is that we forget to remind ourselves that the past wrongs of another relationship do not define the character of our new one! We forget to let go of our past emotional pain and only keep the knowledge of the past experience. We should start out with a refilled trust bucket to share with our new person. Don't put them into a suffering role, not trusting them because of what somebody else did to you. It is just my opinion, but we could save a significant amount of time by starting out our new relationship truthfully.

If you have trust issues you haven't dealt with, be honest about it and give that new person a chance to run, because until you let it go and allow yourself to heal from your pain, you will make every new relationship suffer! I don't mean to be harsh here, but I see it way too often. It is not fair for the new person to be punished for something that they didn't do to you. It may not ever be in the new person's character to ever cheat or lose your trust, but the misery that is put upon them can be devastating. It is not a fair situation to put them in.

If you are a trustworthy person who would never hurt another, allow yourself to imagine what you would feel like if you were accused over and over of something that you would never do. It would drag you down as you defend yourself trying to prove that the other person is wrong.

It is important for you to recognize this and take ownership of this pain you have inside. You must find a way to refill what is empty and allow yourself to have that healthy relationship that you are desiring. Again, you must release this cart of baggage you choose to haul around behind you. It is holding you back from a true loving experience.

No longer will you point fingers and take your emotional experiences out on another person. They are yours to sort out and learn something from. Do it, then you can move forward. Keep a vigilant eye on yourself, for the things we often fear the most are the things we manifest around us to experience again and again. Your awareness of this will help you break your own cycles of attracting the same emotional and dysfunctional lessons again into your next relationship.

~~~

I have these scars

I don't let them define me

A visual reminder

Of what lies behind me

What I have lived through

Where I have been

The sight of them reflects

The strength I have within

~40~

MEANING

Can you teach me the meaning of this life?
I've been struck by the light, not once, but twice.
Will you teach me the meaning of my life?
I need you to show me how I survive.
I was burned on the inside, thrown to the ground,
Lifted straight up, then I turned around.
The colors engulfed me, souls there were many
All were a part of my former life.
I was shown my past, every detail was clear.
Filled my soul overflowing, with love and no fear.
When the vision was over, I opened my eyes,
Everything in my mind, seemed victimized.
Nothing made sense, I felt so alone.
I needed some help to find my way home.
I'm running in circles, can't find the right door.
Not even sure if I'm worth fighting for.
When over my shoulder, I heard Him say:

(I heard God say)

I will teach you, do not be afraid.
I know that you're worth it,
so I'll give you your strength.
I can teach you to find a way.
Always remember,
you were never alone.
I've been standing beside you,
so you could live on.

This is obviously self-explanatory, how fragmented my mind and body felt after an extreme hit from a bolt of lightning. I definitely have very vivid memories from my time on the other side. I know that I was not alone, there were many souls to greet me. Some I recognized, but others were an inner knowing of who they were. Each experience of my life was shown to me. It was a maze of dots connecting the map of my life, the journey I had chosen to walk and gather my life experiences from. It was my book of life. The realization of every connection finally made so much sense to the outcome of my story. I was not afraid to be standing there waiting to fully cross over because I was in the realm of divine peace. I had no pain. I had no baggage. I had no desire of wanting to be anywhere else. I was home! Nothing below me mattered anymore. I was free of the sadness, the pain, and the emotional heartache that defined so much of my life. I was ready to take my final step into my afterlife with a heart full to overflowing with love, peace, and a knowing that I had survived a devastating path of existence. I had completed all that I had been born to do, or so I thought.

The choice became mine as I stood before God, Our Divine, Great Spirit. I let His light of love engulf my soul to its deepest depths. As humans, we have no idea how great this loving energy is until we return in our own light of afterlife. Then, the memory of it reenters you and completes the journey of where you just came from.

As I finished my refueling and view of my life, I knew I was ready to go. However, my choice was placed before me. I was needed. God knew that I was a soul who could share my pain with others and help them find their healing path. Reroute their personal pain and turn them in a new direction of healing. So I came back to do just that. I denied myself my final step over and returned to live out my meant to be moments of life. My intention is clear as my journey carries me to many different destinations to help so many. As I have said before, my return journey would have been worth it, just to help one person.

I hope you take what you need from this as it is just my life experiences that I am sharing with you. My hope is that you can find just one thing to place your mind and soul onto the healing path, for you. I wish you all great success as you endeavor upon your new journey of you.

~~~

Follow your heart.
You will be guided
with the best intentions
of where you are headed.
Trust your instincts
on what you know
you should be doing.
I believe that once a person feels
their passion in something,
then great things fall into place
to lead you into that
spiritual realm of your existence.
Walk softly and be aware
of who surrounds you.
Some will have your back.
Others, may try to derail you.
This is a lesson in life
that we may have to face
on the journey

Remind yourself that you are made in the image of God, The Creator, The Great Spirit above. So, when you doubt yourself, you are doubting Him. It is time to stop doubting yourself and worrying about everything. You need to have faith. You cannot have faith and worry at the same time. They are a contradiction of each other.

AUTHOR'S NOTE

I hope that I have helped you gather a few tools on this journey of life lessons for living. I know that the biggest lesson that I have learned is that I have made my lessons much harder than they ever had to be. I have sabotaged my own progress for simply not having the knowledge or faith to trust that where I was going is where I knew I was meant to be.

As you set forth in your new adventure to find who you are meant to be, do not allow yourself to fail and please, do not sabotage you own progress. Remember, you only need to take baby steps to get to where you are going. Have faith that you are walking into the new you, your true destiny. Find the passion inside you and it will lead you to your purpose. Every one of us has a purpose with a plan. Feel it, from the depths of your soul. Let nothing hold you back from achieving it. It is true that God hasn't yet created a nobody. It is just that He left the choices of the somebody that you want to become, up to you. Give yourself some credit, after all, you have survived your life journey thus far.

Do yourself a favor, close your eyes and picture yourself pulling over to the side of the road. You are now getting out of your form of transportation. Walk back to the rear of your vehicle. Look at the cart that you have been hauling around with you. It is full and overflowing with all the baggage you have allowed yourself to gather and hold onto up to this point of your life. I want you to look at your stuff. I want you to sort out the details of what you have learned and I want you to take a survey of the tools. The tools that were your lessons, the lessons that you learned the most from. Gather only five of them. Put them into your backpack, satchel, or designer piece of luggage, whatever is right for you. Now, unhook your cart from your form of transportation. You will no longer waste your energy carrying that cart around with you. Leave it right there on the side of your road. You now have the tools that you need to move forward on your journey. As you progress you can revisit your cart and gather new tools that may be needed for your next experience in life. What you need to remember is that you will always be able to revisit the memories, they are yours, but you do not need to carry the baggage from those memories around with you any longer. The memories collected from each of your experiences are what give you the tools as a directional map of sorts to guide you and help you understand the purpose of your lesson. There is no more need to repeat the same lessons over and over again. You have the tools for your new adventurous lesson right in your bag. Remember to use them.

Have faith in where you are going from here. Just by acknowledging that you are ready to get your life back on the path that you are meant to be walking your doors will start opening to you. The keys will be in your hand. New beginnings and new blessings will be possible for you. Realize that you are on a personal journey to be a better you. Your changes must start within your own thoughts. Fill your fear space with faith and confidence. Be prepared to meet the new you.

I wish you so much peace, love, and light on your journey, for I too know what it is to begin again. Having never taken the easy road, I can tell you that really learning to live your life is such a tremendously, beautiful thing.

I look forward to sharing another chapter in life with you as I will continue to elaborate more of what I have learned from my time on the other side with God in my next book. Remember I did not regain my strength overnight. Redefining yourself takes patience, so let's take this walk together one breath, one moment, and one fabulous accomplishment at a time.

~~~

One who enters my life through the course of fate shall be

looked at as a gift from above, one that I shall cherish and

celebrate the honor of crossing paths with.

READER'S NOTES:

READER'S NOTES:

READER'S NOTES:

READER'S NOTES:

READER'S NOTES:

READER'S NOTES:

READER'S NOTES:

READER'S NOTES:

READER'S NOTES: